Mometrix

TEST PREPARATION

Court Reporter Exam Secrets Study Guide

DEAR FUTURE EXAM SUCCESS STORY

First of all, **THANK YOU** for purchasing Mometrix study materials!

Second, congratulations! You are one of the few determined test-takers who are committed to doing whatever it takes to excel on your exam. **You have come to the right place.** We developed these study materials with one goal in mind: to deliver you the information you need in a format that's concise and easy to use.

In addition to optimizing your guide for the content of the test, we've outlined our recommended steps for breaking down the preparation process into small, attainable goals so you can make sure you stay on track.

We've also analyzed the entire test-taking process, identifying the most common pitfalls and showing how you can overcome them and be ready for any curveball the test throws you.

Standardized testing is one of the biggest obstacles on your road to success, which only increases the importance of doing well in the high-pressure, high-stakes environment of test day. Your results on this test could have a significant impact on your future, and this guide provides the information and practical advice to help you achieve your full potential on test day.

Your success is our success

We would love to hear from you! If you would like to share the story of your exam success or if you have any questions or comments in regard to our products, please contact us at **800-673-8175** or **support@mometrix.com**.

Thanks again for your business and we wish you continued success!

Sincerely,
The Mometrix Test Preparation Team

Need more help? Check out our flashcards at:
http://MometrixFlashcards.com/CourtReporter

Written and edited by the Mometrix Exam Secrets Test Prep Team
Printed in the United States of America

TABLE OF CONTENTS

Introduction

Thank you for purchasing this resource! You have made the choice to prepare yourself for a test that could have a huge impact on your future, and this guide is designed to help you be fully ready for test day. Obviously, it's important to have a solid understanding of the test material, but you also need to be prepared for the unique environment and stressors of the test, so that you can perform to the best of your abilities.

For this purpose, the first section that appears in this guide is the **Secret Keys**. We've devoted countless hours to meticulously researching what works and what doesn't, and we've boiled down our findings to the five most impactful steps you can take to improve your performance on the test. We start at the beginning with study planning and move through the preparation process, all the way to the testing strategies that will help you get the most out of what you know when you're finally sitting in front of the test.

We recommend that you start preparing for your test as far in advance as possible. However, if you've bought this guide as a last-minute study resource and only have a few days before your test, we recommend that you skip over the first two Secret Keys since they address a long-term study plan.

If you struggle with **test anxiety**, we strongly encourage you to check out our recommendations for how you can overcome it. Test anxiety is a formidable foe, but it can be beaten, and we want to make sure you have the tools you need to defeat it.

Secret Key #1 – Plan Big, Study Small

There's a lot riding on your performance. If you want to ace this test, you're going to need to keep your skills sharp and the material fresh in your mind. You need a plan that lets you review everything you need to know while still fitting in your schedule. We'll break this strategy down into three categories.

Information Organization

Start with the information you already have: the official test outline. From this, you can make a complete list of all the concepts you need to cover before the test. Organize these concepts into groups that can be studied together, and create a list of any related vocabulary you need to learn so you can brush up on any difficult terms. You'll want to keep this vocabulary list handy once you actually start studying since you may need to add to it along the way.

Time Management

Once you have your set of study concepts, decide how to spread them out over the time you have left before the test. Break your study plan into small, clear goals so you have a manageable task for each day and know exactly what you're doing. Then just focus on one small step at a time. When you manage your time this way, you don't need to spend hours at a time studying. Studying a small block of content for a short period each day helps you retain information better and avoid stressing over how much you have left to do. You can relax knowing that you have a plan to cover everything in time. In order for this strategy to be effective though, you have to start studying early and stick to your schedule. Avoid the exhaustion and futility that comes from last-minute cramming!

Study Environment

The environment you study in has a big impact on your learning. Studying in a coffee shop, while probably more enjoyable, is not likely to be as fruitful as studying in a quiet room. It's important to keep distractions to a minimum. You're only planning to study for a short block of time, so make the most of it. Don't pause to check your phone or get up to find a snack. It's also important to **avoid multitasking**. Research has consistently shown that multitasking will make your studying dramatically less effective. Your study area should also be comfortable and well-lit so you don't have the distraction of straining your eyes or sitting on an uncomfortable chair.

The time of day you study is also important. You want to be rested and alert. Don't wait until just before bedtime. Study when you'll be most likely to comprehend and remember. Even better, if you know what time of day your test will be, set that time aside for study. That way your brain will be used to working on that subject at that specific time and you'll have a better chance of recalling information.

Finally, it can be helpful to team up with others who are studying for the same test. Your actual studying should be done in as isolated an environment as possible, but the work of organizing the information and setting up the study plan can be divided up. In between study sessions, you can discuss with your teammates the concepts that you're all studying and quiz each other on the details. Just be sure that your teammates are as serious about the test as you are. If you find that your study time is being replaced with social time, you might need to find a new team.

Secret Key #2 – Make Your Studying Count

You're devoting a lot of time and effort to preparing for this test, so you want to be absolutely certain it will pay off. This means doing more than just reading the content and hoping you can remember it on test day. It's important to make every minute of study count. There are two main areas you can focus on to make your studying count.

Retention

It doesn't matter how much time you study if you can't remember the material. You need to make sure you are retaining the concepts. To check your retention of the information you're learning, try recalling it at later times with minimal prompting. Try carrying around flashcards and glance at one or two from time to time or ask a friend who's also studying for the test to quiz you.

To enhance your retention, look for ways to put the information into practice so that you can apply it rather than simply recalling it. If you're using the information in practical ways, it will be much easier to remember. Similarly, it helps to solidify a concept in your mind if you're not only reading it to yourself but also explaining it to someone else. Ask a friend to let you teach them about a concept you're a little shaky on (or speak aloud to an imaginary audience if necessary). As you try to summarize, define, give examples, and answer your friend's questions, you'll understand the concepts better and they will stay with you longer. Finally, step back for a big picture view and ask yourself how each piece of information fits with the whole subject. When you link the different concepts together and see them working together as a whole, it's easier to remember the individual components.

Finally, practice showing your work on any multi-step problems, even if you're just studying. Writing out each step you take to solve a problem will help solidify the process in your mind, and you'll be more likely to remember it during the test.

Modality

Modality simply refers to the means or method by which you study. Choosing a study modality that fits your own individual learning style is crucial. No two people learn best in exactly the same way, so it's important to know your strengths and use them to your advantage.

For example, if you learn best by visualization, focus on visualizing a concept in your mind and draw an image or a diagram. Try color-coding your notes, illustrating them, or creating symbols that will trigger your mind to recall a learned concept. If you learn best by hearing or discussing information, find a study partner who learns the same way or read aloud to yourself. Think about how to put the information in your own words. Imagine that you are giving a lecture on the topic and record yourself so you can listen to it later.

For any learning style, flashcards can be helpful. Organize the information so you can take advantage of spare moments to review. Underline key words or phrases. Use different colors for different categories. Mnemonic devices (such as creating a short list in which every item starts with the same letter) can also help with retention. Find what works best for you and use it to store the information in your mind most effectively and easily.

Secret Key #3 – Practice the Right Way

Your success on test day depends not only on how many hours you put into preparing, but also on whether you prepared the right way. It's good to check along the way to see if your studying is paying off. One of the most effective ways to do this is by taking practice tests to evaluate your progress. Practice tests are useful because they show exactly where you need to improve. Every time you take a practice test, pay special attention to these three groups of questions:

- The questions you got wrong
- The questions you had to guess on, even if you guessed right
- The questions you found difficult or slow to work through

This will show you exactly what your weak areas are, and where you need to devote more study time. Ask yourself why each of these questions gave you trouble. Was it because you didn't understand the material? Was it because you didn't remember the vocabulary? Do you need more repetitions on this type of question to build speed and confidence? Dig into those questions and figure out how you can strengthen your weak areas as you go back to review the material.

Additionally, many practice tests have a section explaining the answer choices. It can be tempting to read the explanation and think that you now have a good understanding of the concept. However, an explanation likely only covers part of the question's broader context. Even if the explanation makes perfect sense, **go back and investigate** every concept related to the question until you're positive you have a thorough understanding.

As you go along, keep in mind that the practice test is just that: practice. Memorizing these questions and answers will not be very helpful on the actual test because it is unlikely to have any of the same exact questions. If you only know the right answers to the sample questions, you won't be prepared for the real thing. **Study the concepts** until you understand them fully, and then you'll be able to answer any question that shows up on the test.

It's important to wait on the practice tests until you're ready. If you take a test on your first day of study, you may be overwhelmed by the amount of material covered and how much you need to learn. Work up to it gradually.

On test day, you'll need to be prepared for answering questions, managing your time, and using the test-taking strategies you've learned. It's a lot to balance, like a mental marathon that will have a big impact on your future. Like training for a marathon, you'll need to start slowly and work your way up. When test day arrives, you'll be ready.

Start with the strategies you've read in the first two Secret Keys—plan your course and study in the way that works best for you. If you have time, consider using multiple study resources to get different approaches to the same concepts. It can be helpful to see difficult concepts from more than one angle. Then find a good source for practice tests. Many times, the test website will suggest potential study resources or provide sample tests.

Practice Test Strategy

If you're able to find at least three practice tests, we recommend this strategy:

UNTIMED AND OPEN-BOOK PRACTICE

Take the first test with no time constraints and with your notes and study guide handy. Take your time and focus on applying the strategies you've learned.

TIMED AND OPEN-BOOK PRACTICE

Take the second practice test open-book as well, but set a timer and practice pacing yourself to finish in time.

TIMED AND CLOSED-BOOK PRACTICE

Take any other practice tests as if it were test day. Set a timer and put away your study materials. Sit at a table or desk in a quiet room, imagine yourself at the testing center, and answer questions as quickly and accurately as possible.

Keep repeating timed and closed-book tests on a regular basis until you run out of practice tests or it's time for the actual test. Your mind will be ready for the schedule and stress of test day, and you'll be able to focus on recalling the material you've learned.

Secret Key #4 – Pace Yourself

Once you're fully prepared for the material on the test, your biggest challenge on test day will be managing your time. Just knowing that the clock is ticking can make you panic even if you have plenty of time left. Work on pacing yourself so you can build confidence against the time constraints of the exam. Pacing is a difficult skill to master, especially in a high-pressure environment, so **practice is vital**.

Set time expectations for your pace based on how much time is available. For example, if a section has 60 questions and the time limit is 30 minutes, you know you have to average 30 seconds or less per question in order to answer them all. Although 30 seconds is the hard limit, set 25 seconds per question as your goal, so you reserve extra time to spend on harder questions. When you budget extra time for the harder questions, you no longer have any reason to stress when those questions take longer to answer.

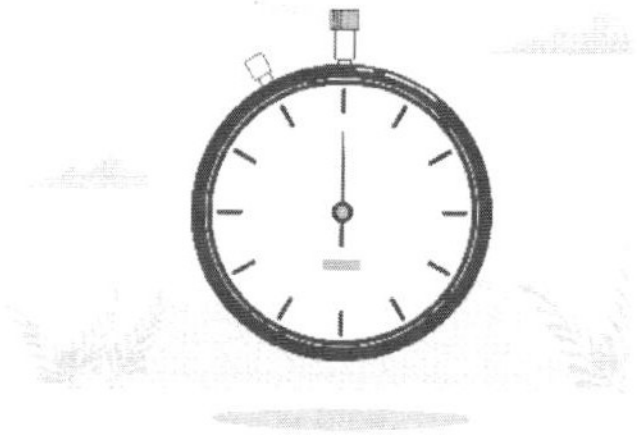

Don't let this time expectation distract you from working through the test at a calm, steady pace, but keep it in mind so you don't spend too much time on any one question. Recognize that taking extra time on one question you don't understand may keep you from answering two that you do understand later in the test. If your time limit for a question is up and you're still not sure of the answer, mark it and move on, and come back to it later if the time and the test format allow. If the testing format doesn't allow you to return to earlier questions, just make an educated guess; then put it out of your mind and move on.

On the easier questions, be careful not to rush. It may seem wise to hurry through them so you have more time for the challenging ones, but it's not worth missing one if you know the concept and just didn't take the time to read the question fully. Work efficiently but make sure you understand the question and have looked at all of the answer choices, since more than one may seem right at first.

Even if you're paying attention to the time, you may find yourself a little behind at some point. You should speed up to get back on track, but do so wisely. Don't panic; just take a few seconds less on each question until you're caught up. Don't guess without thinking, but do look through the answer choices and eliminate any you know are wrong. If you can get down to two choices, it is often worthwhile to guess from those. Once you've chosen an answer, move on and don't dwell on any that you skipped or had to hurry through. If a question was taking too long, chances are it was one of the harder ones, so you weren't as likely to get it right anyway.

On the other hand, if you find yourself getting ahead of schedule, it may be beneficial to slow down a little. The more quickly you work, the more likely you are to make a careless mistake that will affect your score. You've budgeted time for each question, so don't be afraid to spend that time. Practice an efficient but careful pace to get the most out of the time you have.

Secret Key #5 – Have a Plan for Guessing

When you're taking the test, you may find yourself stuck on a question. Some of the answer choices seem better than others, but you don't see the one answer choice that is obviously correct. What do you do?

The scenario described above is very common, yet most test takers have not effectively prepared for it. Developing and practicing a plan for guessing may be one of the single most effective uses of your time as you get ready for the exam.

In developing your plan for guessing, there are three questions to address:

- When should you start the guessing process?
- How should you narrow down the choices?
- Which answer should you choose?

When to Start the Guessing Process

Unless your plan for guessing is to select C every time (which, despite its merits, is not what we recommend), you need to leave yourself enough time to apply your answer elimination strategies. Since you have a limited amount of time for each question, that means that if you're going to give yourself the best shot at guessing correctly, you have to decide quickly whether or not you will guess.

Of course, the best-case scenario is that you don't have to guess at all, so first, see if you can answer the question based on your knowledge of the subject and basic reasoning skills. Focus on the key words in the question and try to jog your memory of related topics. Give yourself a chance to bring the knowledge to mind, but once you realize that you don't have (or you can't access) the knowledge you need to answer the question, it's time to start the guessing process.

It's almost always better to start the guessing process too early than too late. It only takes a few seconds to remember something and answer the question from knowledge. Carefully eliminating wrong answer choices takes longer. Plus, going through the process of eliminating answer choices can actually help jog your memory.

Summary: Start the guessing process as soon as you decide that you can't answer the question based on your knowledge.

How to Narrow Down the Choices

The next chapter in this book (**Test-Taking Strategies**) includes a wide range of strategies for how to approach questions and how to look for answer choices to eliminate. You will definitely want to read those carefully, practice them, and figure out which ones work best for you. Here though, we're going to address a mindset rather than a particular strategy.

Your odds of guessing an answer correctly depend on how many options you are choosing from.

Number of options left	5	4	3	2	1
Odds of guessing correctly	20%	25%	33%	50%	100%

You can see from this chart just how valuable it is to be able to eliminate incorrect answers and make an educated guess, but there are two things that many test takers do that cause them to miss out on the benefits of guessing:

- Accidentally eliminating the correct answer
- Selecting an answer based on an impression

We'll look at the first one here, and the second one in the next section.

To avoid accidentally eliminating the correct answer, we recommend a thought exercise called **the $5 challenge**. In this challenge, you only eliminate an answer choice from contention if you are willing to bet $5 on it being wrong. Why $5? Five dollars is a small but not insignificant amount of money. It's an amount you could afford to lose but wouldn't want to throw away. And while losing $5 once might not hurt too much, doing it twenty times will set you back $100. In the same way, each small decision you make—eliminating a choice here, guessing on a question there—won't by itself impact your score very much, but when you put them all together, they can make a big difference. By holding each answer choice elimination decision to a higher standard, you can reduce the risk of accidentally eliminating the correct answer.

The $5 challenge can also be applied in a positive sense: If you are willing to bet $5 that an answer choice *is* correct, go ahead and mark it as correct.

Summary: Only eliminate an answer choice if you are willing to bet $5 that it is wrong.

Which Answer to Choose

You're taking the test. You've run into a hard question and decided you'll have to guess. You've eliminated all the answer choices you're willing to bet $5 on. Now you have to pick an answer. Why do we even need to talk about this? Why can't you just pick whichever one you feel like when the time comes?

The answer to these questions is that if you don't come into the test with a plan, you'll rely on your impression to select an answer choice, and if you do that, you risk falling into a trap. The test writers know that everyone who takes their test will be guessing on some of the questions, so they intentionally write wrong answer choices to seem plausible. You still have to pick an answer though, and if the wrong answer choices are designed to look right, how can you ever be sure that you're not falling for their trap? The best solution we've found to this dilemma is to take the decision out of your hands entirely. Here is the process we recommend:

Once you've eliminated any choices that you are confident (willing to bet $5) are wrong, select the first remaining choice as your answer.

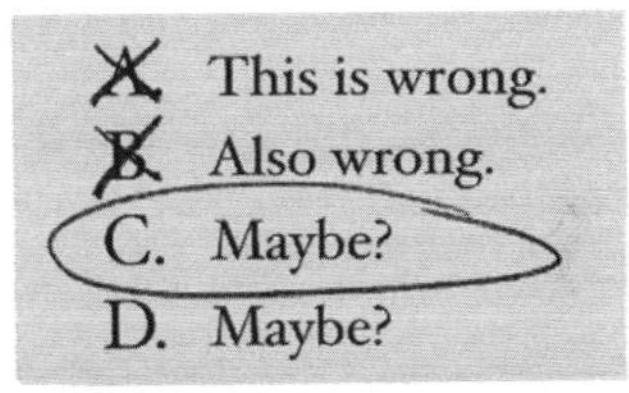

Whether you choose to select the first remaining choice, the second, or the last, the important thing is that you use some preselected standard. Using this approach guarantees that you will not be enticed into selecting an answer choice that looks right, because you are not basing your decision on how the answer choices look.

This is not meant to make you question your knowledge. Instead, it is to help you recognize the difference between your knowledge and your impressions. There's a huge difference between thinking an answer is right because of what you know, and thinking an answer is right because it looks or sounds like it should be right.

Summary: To ensure that your selection is appropriately random, make a predetermined selection from among all answer choices you have not eliminated.

Test-Taking Strategies

This section contains a list of test-taking strategies that you may find helpful as you work through the test. By taking what you know and applying logical thought, you can maximize your chances of answering any question correctly!

It is very important to realize that every question is different and every person is different: no single strategy will work on every question, and no single strategy will work for every person. That's why we've included all of them here, so you can try them out and determine which ones work best for different types of questions and which ones work best for you.

Question Strategies

✓ Read Carefully

Read the question and the answer choices carefully. Don't miss the question because you misread the terms. You have plenty of time to read each question thoroughly and make sure you understand what is being asked. Yet a happy medium must be attained, so don't waste too much time. You must read carefully and efficiently.

✓ Contextual Clues

Look for contextual clues. If the question includes a word you are not familiar with, look at the immediate context for some indication of what the word might mean. Contextual clues can often give you all the information you need to decipher the meaning of an unfamiliar word. Even if you can't determine the meaning, you may be able to narrow down the possibilities enough to make a solid guess at the answer to the question.

✓ Prefixes

If you're having trouble with a word in the question or answer choices, try dissecting it. Take advantage of every clue that the word might include. Prefixes can be a huge help. Usually, they allow you to determine a basic meaning. *Pre-* means before, *post-* means after, *pro-* is positive, *de-* is negative. From prefixes, you can get an idea of the general meaning of the word and try to put it into context.

✓ Hedge Words

Watch out for critical hedge words, such as *likely, may, can, often, almost, mostly, usually, generally, rarely,* and *sometimes.* Question writers insert these hedge phrases to cover every possibility. Often an answer choice will be wrong simply because it leaves no room for exception. Be on guard for answer choices that have definitive words such as *exactly* and *always.*

✓ Switchback Words

Stay alert for *switchbacks.* These are the words and phrases frequently used to alert you to shifts in thought. The most common switchback words are *but, although,* and *however.* Others include *nevertheless, on the other hand, even though, while, in spite of, despite,* and *regardless of.* Switchback words are important to catch because they can change the direction of the question or an answer choice.

✓ FACE VALUE

When in doubt, use common sense. Accept the situation in the problem at face value. Don't read too much into it. These problems will not require you to make wild assumptions. If you have to go beyond creativity and warp time or space in order to have an answer choice fit the question, then you should move on and consider the other answer choices. These are normal problems rooted in reality. The applicable relationship or explanation may not be readily apparent, but it is there for you to figure out. Use your common sense to interpret anything that isn't clear.

Answer Choice Strategies

✓ ANSWER SELECTION

The most thorough way to pick an answer choice is to identify and eliminate wrong answers until only one is left, then confirm it is the correct answer. Sometimes an answer choice may immediately seem right, but be careful. The test writers will usually put more than one reasonable answer choice on each question, so take a second to read all of them and make sure that the other choices are not equally obvious. As long as you have time left, it is better to read every answer choice than to pick the first one that looks right without checking the others.

✓ ANSWER CHOICE FAMILIES

An answer choice family consists of two (in rare cases, three) answer choices that are very similar in construction and cannot all be true at the same time. If you see two answer choices that are direct opposites or parallels, one of them is usually the correct answer. For instance, if one answer choice says that quantity *x* increases and another either says that quantity *x* decreases (opposite) or says that quantity *y* increases (parallel), then those answer choices would fall into the same family. An answer choice that doesn't match the construction of the answer choice family is more likely to be incorrect. Most questions will not have answer choice families, but when they do appear, you should be prepared to recognize them.

✓ ELIMINATE ANSWERS

Eliminate answer choices as soon as you realize they are wrong, but make sure you consider all possibilities. If you are eliminating answer choices and realize that the last one you are left with is also wrong, don't panic. Start over and consider each choice again. There may be something you missed the first time that you will realize on the second pass.

✓ AVOID FACT TRAPS

Don't be distracted by an answer choice that is factually true but doesn't answer the question. You are looking for the choice that answers the question. Stay focused on what the question is asking for so you don't accidentally pick an answer that is true but incorrect. Always go back to the question and make sure the answer choice you've selected actually answers the question and is not merely a true statement.

✓ EXTREME STATEMENTS

In general, you should avoid answers that put forth extreme actions as standard practice or proclaim controversial ideas as established fact. An answer choice that states the "process should be used in certain situations, if..." is much more likely to be correct than one that states the "process should be discontinued completely." The first is a calm rational statement and doesn't even make a definitive, uncompromising stance, using a hedge word *if* to provide wiggle room, whereas the second choice is far more extreme.

☑ BENCHMARK

As you read through the answer choices and you come across one that seems to answer the question well, mentally select that answer choice. This is not your final answer, but it's the one that will help you evaluate the other answer choices. The one that you selected is your benchmark or standard for judging each of the other answer choices. Every other answer choice must be compared to your benchmark. That choice is correct until proven otherwise by another answer choice beating it. If you find a better answer, then that one becomes your new benchmark. Once you've decided that no other choice answers the question as well as your benchmark, you have your final answer.

☑ PREDICT THE ANSWER

Before you even start looking at the answer choices, it is often best to try to predict the answer. When you come up with the answer on your own, it is easier to avoid distractions and traps because you will know exactly what to look for. The right answer choice is unlikely to be word-for-word what you came up with, but it should be a close match. Even if you are confident that you have the right answer, you should still take the time to read each option before moving on.

General Strategies

☑ TOUGH QUESTIONS

If you are stumped on a problem or it appears too hard or too difficult, don't waste time. Move on! Remember though, if you can quickly check for obviously incorrect answer choices, your chances of guessing correctly are greatly improved. Before you completely give up, at least try to knock out a couple of possible answers. Eliminate what you can and then guess at the remaining answer choices before moving on.

☑ CHECK YOUR WORK

Since you will probably not know every term listed and the answer to every question, it is important that you get credit for the ones that you do know. Don't miss any questions through careless mistakes. If at all possible, try to take a second to look back over your answer selection and make sure you've selected the correct answer choice and haven't made a costly careless mistake (such as marking an answer choice that you didn't mean to mark). This quick double check should more than pay for itself in caught mistakes for the time it costs.

☑ PACE YOURSELF

It's easy to be overwhelmed when you're looking at a page full of questions; your mind is confused and full of random thoughts, and the clock is ticking down faster than you would like. Calm down and maintain the pace that you have set for yourself. Especially as you get down to the last few minutes of the test, don't let the small numbers on the clock make you panic. As long as you are on track by monitoring your pace, you are guaranteed to have time for each question.

☑ DON'T RUSH

It is very easy to make errors when you are in a hurry. Maintaining a fast pace in answering questions is pointless if it makes you miss questions that you would have gotten right otherwise. Test writers like to include distracting information and wrong answers that seem right. Taking a little extra time to avoid careless mistakes can make all the difference in your test score. Find a pace that allows you to be confident in the answers that you select.

⊘ Keep Moving

Panicking will not help you pass the test, so do your best to stay calm and keep moving. Taking deep breaths and going through the answer elimination steps you practiced can help to break through a stress barrier and keep your pace.

Final Notes

The combination of a solid foundation of content knowledge and the confidence that comes from practicing your plan for applying that knowledge is the key to maximizing your performance on test day. As your foundation of content knowledge is built up and strengthened, you'll find that the strategies included in this chapter become more and more effective in helping you quickly sift through the distractions and traps of the test to isolate the correct answer.

Now that you're preparing to move forward into the test content chapters of this book, be sure to keep your goal in mind. As you read, think about how you will be able to apply this information on the test. If you've already seen sample questions for the test and you have an idea of the question format and style, try to come up with questions of your own that you can answer based on what you're reading. This will give you valuable practice applying your knowledge in the same ways you can expect to on test day.

Good luck and good studying!

Reporting Practices

Certification Program

The certification program first began in 1935. By the 1970s, a nationally acclaimed certification program was initiated. This test recognized the mechanical and intellectual skills of entry-level reporters. In December of 1995, NCRA had members amounting to 13,000 registered professional reporters. Certification for register professional reporters, registered merit reporters, and registered diplomat reporters can be obtained through NCRA certification programs. The other certification programs which NCRA gives includes: certified reporting instructor, certified legal video specialists, and certified real-time reporter. The careful analysis of job specifications is an integral part of the test. Furthermore, NCRA uses a professional examination service to build test questions based on the goals that a reporter must meet. A test advisory committee assigns each question, a rating to determine if the test question is appropriate for the exams.

NCRA's Certification Program History

Each state has the obligation to protect the public community's well-being, safety, and interests. With that in mind, five guidelines were regulated. The reasons for certification can be found in these five guidelines: the public community may suffer from exposed risks in the areas of life, health, safety or finances associated with unregulated practice of the profession; the job performance demands that the person be skilled, knowledgeable, and trained in order to achieve the tasks or goals associated with the occupation; the person performing the task must use judgment on an independent level; the occupation stands out in a noticeable way from other licensed or other unlicensed professionals; the financial standpoint of regulating the group of professionals is warranted. Certification increases proficiency and qualifications of the persons being tested. The persons' knowledge and skills are specifically defined during the certification process.

Importance of the Certification Process

The two most important principles surrounding certification include increasing the qualifications of the reporters through an exam and to ensure the commitment of the reporter to lifelong learning. The benefits of certification for a reporter can enhance admiration, recognition, integrity, know-how, and skill. Also, the reporter increases his opportunities for job advancement. Certification allows a high level of credibility to the reporter's work. This level of credibility is communicated to the judges and state-funded attorneys on a daily basis. Excessive costs and time delays can be occurred where reporting skills do not meet the demands of the job. A 1993 survey of 600 randomly selected participants, valued testing on an individual basis at a rate of 81%. Participants obtained their certification for reasons of professionalism, at the urging of supervisors or teachers, to obtain employment, to increase finances, to gain personal gratification, and to increase work options in multiple states.

Importance of Continuing Education

In a 1993 survey, 85% of the reporters surveyed indicated that they believed that it should be mandatory for court reporters to continue with their educational pursuits. The reporter needs continuing education in order to stay technologically aware, to gain new information, to gain updated and correct information, to maintain skills and proficiency, to gain confidence, to be more valuable and balanced in the workplace, and to master precise skill levels. In the 1995 survey, "A Study of Employment Prospects for Court Reporters", the following was determined: reporters gain more opportunities for employment in freelance work; and the end CRA certification allows reporters increased opportunities for employment. The Bureau of Labor Statistics reports that there is rising competition for entry-level court reporting positions. Certification should increase the reporter's ability to compete and to advance in entry-level jobs within the legal community.

Registered Professional Reporter Exam

The written knowledge exam is 90 minutes long. The exam has 100 questions in a multiple choice format. A passing score is considered to be 70% or more. There are 48 reporting questions. There are 44 transcript production questions, 4 operating practice questions, and 4 professional issues and continuing education questions. A recorded dictation tape is used as part of the skills section of the test. Each part is called a leg of a test. Each leg or section can last five minutes with one minute of warm up questions. In total passing scores for literary matter at 180 wpm, jury charge at 200 wpm, and voice testimony at 225 wpm totaling 3 1/2 hours for transcription. The RPR skills test must receive a graded score of 95%. Passing exams is expected and necessary in the performance of the duties of court reporters.

Registered Merit Reporter Exam

The written knowledge exam is 90 minutes long. The exam has 100 questions in a multiple choice format. A passing score for the written knowledge test is considered to be 70% or more. The test is divided into four parts. There are 47 reporting questions. There are 41 transcript production questions, six administration questions, six professional issues, and continuing education questions. The RMR skills test has three parts. A recorded dictation tape is used as part of the skills section of the test. The test does not have to be completed in one sitting. 1 1/4 hours are needed to complete each transcription leg or section. A score of 95% is considered passing in each part of the skill test sections. The RMR skills test includes literary matter at 200 wpm, jury charge in 240 wpm, and 2 voice testimonies at 260 wpm.

Eligibility Requirements for the NCRA Certification

Only fully paid members of the NCRA are permitted to take the RPR exam. Membership dues must be paid in full by January 31 for the May examination date. Membership dues must be paid in full by July 31 for the November examination date. Likewise, in order to take the RMR skills test, you must be a fully paid member. Membership dues must be paid in full by July 31 for the November examination date. The eligibility requirements for the RMR WKT are more stringent. The reporter must meet at least one of the following criteria: ongoing status of RPR consisting of a three year period; or an RPR and hold membership of the NCRA ongoing for a period of four years; or an RPR and six years of activity as a reporter; or an RPR and have a bachelor's degree.

RPR and the RMR Certification Differences

The RPR has been designed to provide certification for entry-level reporters. Persons to complete this certification will be qualified to work as professional court reporters. In addition, the RMR certification is indicative of a mastery of certain skills. Merit reporters should have the following skills: management skills, assignment scheduling systems, supply of support staff, equipment acquisition and maintenance, and superior guarantee methods. The professional will have knowledge concerning legal issues concerning confidentiality, guidelines, customs, and ethics in reporting. The professional merit reporter will practice professional conduct at all times. Comprehension gained through association with the NCRA code of professional ethics, local, state, and national reporting associations and pro bono activities with bar associations can enhance the knowledge of the professional reporter. The successful completion of the RPR and the RMR certification requires expertise, proficiency, and aptitude in the profession.

Job Analysis for the Registered Professional Reporter

This job analysis provides information valuable to freelance, official court reporters, reporter educators, court administrators, and the legal profession. This analysis has been provided by the National Court Reporters Association Task Force in cooperation with the professional examination service. This analysis was revised in 1985. The register professional reporter is required to produce a verbatim record of proceedings. The term verbatim refers to an accurate recount of oral and nonverbal exchanges and actions that occurred during the proceedings. The register professional reporter's sphere of influence includes the following: reporting, transcript production, operating practices, professional issues, and continuing education. 48% of the Register National Reporter's work is accomplished with reporting. 44% is accomplished through transcript production. 4% includes practices, such as filing, storage, proper discard of notes, and record compilation. 4% of the work involves professional conduct and ongoing educational efforts.

Aspects of the Reporting

Check the identification information for each document involved in a case. The case documents include dockets, complaints, indictments, information sheets, and notices. The case documents should be identified by description, caption, or style of the case, a case number, jurisdiction and venue. Venue refers to the site or location of the proceeding. The jurisdiction of the case involves the extent of authority or ruling over the case. For example, a judge may have jurisdiction over a certain case. Names, addresses, and titles of counsel, and the counsel's client should be determined through the questioning of counsel or by the presentation of documented proof. Such documented proof can include business cards or pleadings. This aspect of the reporter's duties requires comprehension of court and quasi-judicial systems; familiarity with pleadings and notices; and an understanding of docket systems.

The reporter should be able to create a verbatim record of the words spoken aloud during the presentation of the case. In addition, the verbatim report shall be considered conflict-free. The term conflict-free refers to a reporting system that attempts to be presented without divergence or dispute. This aspect of the reporter's duties requires comprehension of the reporting system; an understanding of English, proper grammar, punctuation usage, correct sentence structure, accurate spelling, and the appropriate use of vocabulary; a familiarity with the role played by the reporter involved in the case proceedings is mandated. In addition, the speaker should be identified. Speeches given simultaneously are reported; the proper use of medical, legal, or technological terminology is given; legal procedures are reported; the verbatim record is written using the proper structure; and the reporter shows skill in using computer-aided transcription equipment.

Creating a Verbatim Report

The reporter should type at speeds of 225 words per minute on a five-minute actual word count. A test using a two-voice testimony is used to determine typing speeds. The reporter should be able to perform with a score of 95% precision rate for the two-voice testimony test. The reporter should type at speeds of 200 words per minute for a length of five minutes on an actual word count test representing a charge to the jury. The test using the charge to the jury should be performed with a score of 95% precision rate. The reporter should type at speeds of 180 words per minute for lengths of five minutes on an actual word-count test of literacy or straight matter. The test consisting of the literacy or straight matter should be performed with a score of 95%.

Reporting Nonverbal Actions

The reporter should create an accurate record of the nonverbal actions that go on during case proceeding. An accurate record will include identification of all participants; the swearing in of a witness under oath; description of the kind of examination given; accurate representation of those present, including the jury or absence of a jury; and conversations that take place off record; the markings of the exhibit or evidence; any recesses or breaks, and indication of time frames in an accurate record of demonstrations or physical actions. The reporter should comprehend the reporting system and be familiar with all legal procedures presented. The reporter will need to be knowledgeable concerning the structure of a verbatim record. The reporter will give an appropriate record of the actions that occur within the proceeding. The reporter will demonstrate the actions of a professional reporter.

Legal Proceeding

Legal proceedings can include the rules of evidence, the statutes, or laws that relate to the case. The reporter must be familiar with the techniques for marking exhibits presented in a case. Exhibits can be marked with sequential numbering or with letters. Marking techniques involve issues concerning the custody and disposition of the exhibits. These rules may limit the availability of exhibits for public inspection. The reporter should understand the difference between marking an exhibit for identification purposes or in marking the exhibit for introduction as evidence. An understanding of the oath or affirmation used and how that affects the jurisdiction of the proceeding is essential. The reporter should comprehend the appropriateness of responses elicited under oath. Certain stipulations may result in the filing or waving of the case, the certification of the case, or the signing or sealing of the case.

Reading Back of Notes and in Transcript Distribution

The reporter reads the notes of the proceeding aloud in a clear and distinct voice. The reporter's voice and manner should be poised and professional. The reporter exhibits a knowledge of the reporting system; medical, legal, and other technical phraseology; marking notes or logs; and timeliness of read back items. The reporter distributes transcripts on the delivery date in appropriate numbers for all participants. The cost involved in the distribution is addressed with the fees for transcript and ancillary services. The distribution or filing is done in relation to the rules, regulations and statues guiding the process. The timely distribution of the transcript is ensured by regular, expedited, overnight, or immediate daily delivery mail postings. The reporter may need to distribute adjunct items in the form of videotapes, ASCII files or other media.

Record Verification Process

The responsibility of the reporter during the record verification process includes making notes for later clarification. In addition, the reporter must make sure that spellings, words, terms, quotations, and citations are accurate. The reporter is responsible for requesting that the information be repeated for accurate documentation of a verbatim record. The reporter must have a good command of the English language, including the use of grammar, punctuation, sentence structure, word spellings, and a strong vocabulary. The reporter is responsible for knowing how a judge may view the policy of interrupting speakers. The reporter's manner of interruption should correspond with a respectful and tactful attitude towards the court and council members. The reporter is efficient, in flagging notes during the proceedings for later review and clarification. The reporter can use reference materials competently to enhance efforts of the verification process.

Transcript Production Process

The reporter makes an information sheet that is used as a guideline to prepare the transcript. The reporter uses his understanding to create a transcript noting the number of copies required, venue, captions, case number, appearances, stipulations, witnesses, exhibits, index, names, terminology, and delivery date. The reporter uses the correct spelling of names and technical terminology as it relates to the case and its proceedings. The information sheet is instrumental in aiding the reporter in the preparation of the final transcripts. The reporter uses the computer to convert and edit shorthand into English. The reporter has a strong command of the English language. The reporter has a strong vocabulary and uses medical, legal, and technical terminology efficiently and accurately. The reporter uses the features of the scoping/text editor on the computer. This allows the reporter to make desired changes.

Computer Aided Transcription and Word Processing

The reporter creates a transcript formatted with an attention to style, margins, title pages, appearances, parenthetical statements, indexes and certificate pages. The reporter uses the word processor or typewriter in conjunction with other reference materials to produce the transcript. Some other reference materials used are the Physicians' Desk Reference, Bartlett's Quotations, telephone books, and equipment manuals. The reporter uses the correct spelling of names and technical terminology as it relates to the case and its proceedings. The reporter has a strong command of the English language and its mechanics. The reporter has a strong vocabulary and uses medical, legal, and technical terminology efficiently and accurately. The reporter can type at speeds of at least six pages per hour on non-technical matters or at a net typing speed of 60 words per minute with accuracy.

Researching Data for the Transcript

The reporter is responsible for the accuracy of the transcript. The reporter must comprehend the subject matter and location of reference material that can be used in the verification process of data. Reference material can be in the form of dictionaries, directories, atlases, newspapers, magazines, books, and case reports. The case reports can be found in the law libraries. The reporter should be familiar with the library reference services and index systems in order to efficiently access the required information. The reporter should be familiar with organizations and associations representing various employment, trades, and careers. The reporter should be familiar with the legal citation structure. The reporter should be cognizant of the information that can be provided from judges, lawyers, and other reporters. The reporter should use research skills to verify the contents of the transcript.

Proofreading the Contents of the Transcript

The reporter has the responsibility of making corrections to the transcript. The mistakes are detected by reading the document aloud. Mistakes can be made from hearing incorrectly, misspelling a word and by mistranslations that occur throughout the proceeding. The reporter must have a strong command of the English language and its mechanics. This includes a strong comprehension and grammar, punctuation, proper sentence structure, and accurate use of vocabulary. The reporter must comprehend medical vocabularies, legal vocabularies, and be familiar with technological phraseologies. The reporter must have fundamental knowledge regarding the transcript format and structure. Proofreading includes an attention to connection in the reading material, sense and detail of the proceedings, recognizing suspect segments of the transcript, flagging transcript notes that require verification, and using punctuation to enhance the meaning of the phrase or group of words.

Operating Practices

The operating practices include filing, storage, the proper disposal of notes, and recordkeeping techniques. A systematic storage is advised for filing and easy retrieval of notes related to a case. The reporter should understand how to classify files to be stored. The filing system should be a secure storage system that allows easy retrieval of notes. Notes can include diaries, calendar entries, and storage logs. The reporter should know and follow strict rules in regards to the proper disposal of notes. Operating practices also includes recordkeeping techniques. The reporter should keep proper business accounts. These accounts will ensure a well-organized functioning system of business. These accounts are necessary in formulating income and expenses for tax purposes. The reporter should adhere to the local, state, and federal government laws. The reporter should keep an appointment book listing reporting assignments.

Professional Issues Regarding the Requirements Maintained by a Reporter

The professional issues and continuing education requirements of the reporter place restrictions upon that reporter's conduct. The reporter that is professional will keep informed concerning customs, procedures, and developments that occur within the reporting industry. One way to keep informed concerning customs, procedures, and developments is to be well read. The reporter takes advantage of information found in special journals, supporting professional reporting associations, and through active participating in events associated with the legal professions. The reporter maintains confidentiality regarding case proceedings. Grand jury proceedings and sealed records are held in the strictest confidence. Conversations with judges, counsel, or other legal personnel are also deemed confidential. The reporter must practice, professional conduct and ethics in relation to their position. A set of laws, customs and policies guide this conduct. The NCRA code of Professional Ethics provides further guidelines.

The local, state, and national professional reporting associations provide guidelines and mandates for the reporter to follow. Many of the reporter's pro bono activities and associations are located within the legal community. The strengths that assist the reporter in this position include punctuality to the workplace and in delivering the transcripts, good manners, dependability, impartiality, and appropriate and timely replies to verbal and in print exchanges of communications. The reporter works diligently to attain the knowledge and work skills that are available through continuing education programs and courses. The reporter can stay on top of new techniques that may impact the vocation of a reporter. Some of these new techniques are taught in classes that offer further instruction on computer-aided transcriptions, videotape and tape recording techniques, and the knowledge and impact made concerning an individual's strengths and weaknesses.

Registered Merit Reporter Job Description as Set Forth by the National Court Reporters Association Task Force

The Registered Merit Reporter's job description includes the maintenance of the job skills associated with a registered professional reporter and the additional skills of the Registered Merit Reporter. The Registered Merit Reporter must maintain a high-level of skill and ability. The reporter must have a competent knowledge of technical proceedings to continue the production of on-time verbatim transcripts. The reporter's use of technology denotes exceptional skills in all forms of reporting devices. The capabilities of the reporter are demonstrated through management skills related the tasks performed by a registered merit reporter. The Registered Merit Reporter can expect a breakdown of the job domain to be delineated as follows: 47% in reporting tasks, 41% in transcript production, 6% in administrative tasks, and 6% in professional issues and continuing educational tasks.

Tasks Performed by a Registered Merit Reporter

The Registered Merit Reporter's tasks are conducted by exchanging oral communication into the written word. The written word is used to create a verbatim record that includes correct punctuation and conflict-free reporting system. The reporter has a strong command of the English language and its mechanics. The reporter uses the correct medical, legal, and technological jargon. The reporter is familiar with all legal procedures and appropriately fulfills the role of the reporter. The computer-aided transcription equipment is used to create a properly formatted verbatim transcript. The five-minute actual workout test is performed at speeds of at least 260 wpm. The five-minute actual workout test of a charge to the jury is performed at speeds of up to at least 240 wpm. The five-minute actual workout test of literacy or straight test is performed at speeds of at least 200 wpm.

The Registered Merit Reporter's tasks include the reporting of the nonverbal exchanges. These nonverbal exchanges include speaker identification, affirmation of witness, types of examinations given by the counsel, the distinction recorded of jury proceedings versus proceedings without the jury present, documentations of off record conversations, appropriate markings of the exhibits, breaks or recesses, and time frames recorded. Any physical prompting such as pointing or exhibitions are documented. The Registered Merit Reporter conscientiously studies the reporting system. The reporter has a clear understanding of the legal procedures that take place during a proceeding. For instance, the rules or evidence or statutes are clearly comprehended by the reporter. A sequential number or letter classification mark exhibits. The reporter is familiar with the techniques used by the court in marking an exhibit.

The Registered Merit Reporter's task includes understanding of the guidelines that are used in marking, custody, and disposition of exhibits. The rules designate those exhibits that are available for open inspection and those that are restricted. Some markings allow the exhibit to be identified while other markings allow the exhibit to be introduced as evidence or proof. The reporter makes record of the oath/affirmation given and makes notes of the jurisdiction or authority that presides over the case. The reporter understands the appropriateness of elicited responses given under oath. The reporter comprehends the stipulations that may impact a case. For instance, waiving of filing, certification, signing and sealing documents are stipulations that can impact the case. The reporter has a clear understanding of the layout of the verbatim record, the reporter's role, and the actions to be taken during a proceeding.

The reporter can competently read the notes of the proceedings with clarity and an audible voice in a confident tone. This performance cannot be accomplished without a thorough knowledge of the reporting method. The reading will be given using the appropriate medical, legal, and technological jargon with proper pronunciations and techniques. The reporter should provide marking notes or a log for the read back task. The reporter will further exhibit competence in reading only the portions that are necessary in a timely manner. The record verification task demands that the reporter have command of the English language and its mechanics. The reporter must use grace and tactfulness during the proceedings. Occasionally, the reporter may need to interrupt provided the judge is not one to take issue with this practice. Flagging notes allows the reporter to achieve clarification and verification later.

The Registered Merit Reporter is comfortable and confident in the use of the computerized equipment for editing. This equipment is used to convert shorthand into English. The reporter has a strong command of the English language and its mechanics. The reporter can effectively use grammar, correct punctuation, appropriate sentence structure, proficient spelling, and has a strong vocabulary. The reporter used medical, legal, and technical jargon in the documents appropriately. The reporter has a strong comprehension of the computer's operations. The reporter is confident in the use of the CRT, keyboard, printer, litigation support, and in telecommunication systems. The reporter can edit the document effectively using the scoping/text features. The reporter uses the proper format in creating transcripts. The reporter can use the reference materials with ease. The reporter can trouble shoot requests or problems associated with the job of a scopist text editor or other supportive personnel.

The reporter has efficient skills in finding reference materials. Reference materials that are useful to a reporter include dictionaries, directories, atlases, newspapers, magazines, books, and case reports located in law libraries. The reporter understands and can effectively use the Library reference indexes. The reporter is knowledgeable about existing groups and associations that stand for a variety of careers, crafts, and vocations. The report has a clear understanding of the legal citation structures. The reporter has a good working support system in place. The reporter gains information from judges, lawyers, and fellow reporters by networking. The reporter is responsible to make corrections that may be detected during a transcript reading. The reporter has a strong command of the English language and its mechanics. The reporter uses correct terminology and punctuation. The reporter careful verifies each section of the document.

The Registered Merit Reporter must provide the correct number of transcript copies, video tapes, and/or computer disks along with the disposition and cost provisions associated with each proceeding. The reporter is cognizant of time frames and deadlines, the actions required in ordering, legal action supports, filing procedures of video tapes or transcripts, fees associated with videotaping, ASCII files, and transcript fees. The reporter understands the link between proper shipping time deadlines and the delivery schedules. The reporter comprehends the means that is required for the delivery of the transcripts to the proper destination in a timely manner. The administrative duties of the reporter include organizing schedules, support staff enlistments, getting the equipment and supplies in place, and record keeping procedures. The reporter also makes sure that the proofreaders, text editors perform with excellence and efficiency.

Professional Requirements of the Registered Merit Reporter

The reporter behaves appropriately for the situation and position that relate to the work of the court environment. The reporter performs in keeping with the custom or traditions required in court. The reporter is continually learning and is considered well-read on professional journals. The reporter demonstrates a strong comprehension of reporting associations and activities involving the legal community. The reporter is helpful to new reporters just starting out in the profession. The reporter maintains a high level of confidentiality in the performing his or her duties. The reporter keeps conversations between, judges, lawyers, and the legal community strictly confidential. The reporter practices a high code of professional and ethical conduct. The reporter maintains the NCRA Code of Professional Conduct to the best of his or her ability. Local, state and national reporting associations provide the reporter with expert information pertinent to the field.

The Registered Merit Reporter is knowledgeable about pro bono activities associated with the bar. The reporter is cognizant of opportunities provided by training and internship prospects. The reporter is aware of how his or her strengths and weaknesses have a direct impact on job performance skills. The reporter assumes the full obligation of creating a verbatim transcription in a timely and efficient manner. The reporter is dependable and courteous in providing documentation of legal proceedings. The reporter creates the oral and written documentation of the case proceedings in an unbiased manner. The reporter comprehends the importance and the content available in continuing education programs. The reporter comprehends the technical developments that are applicable to the position of reporter. The reporter is competent in the use of computer-aided transcription devices, videotape, and tape recording devices. The reporter is aware of his or her strengths and weaknesses.

Equipment Guidelines Used in the Skills Test

The admission ticket given for the test will include a description of the equipment available at the test site. However, the person taking the CAT test should bring CAT writers, software, computers, security keys, blank 3 ½ inch disks, labels for the disk, printers, cables, a minimum 16-foot sized extension cord(s), adapters, and surge protector/ power strips. The person that is using the word processor for the test should check that the site has all necessary equipment on hand. The required items include the monitor, hard drive, software, printer, keyboard, extension cord(s), surge protectors, and electrical adapters. The person using the typewriter should carry their own typewriter to the test site. The test person assumes the total responsibility of the use of the equipment provided at the site or brought to the site by the test person.

Test Equipment Guidelines to Be Used in the Skills Test

The test person will not be given assistance in the operation of any device. The risk of ill performing equipment, damaged, stolen, or other unfortunate circumstances that may occur to the equipment is solely the responsibility of the test taker. The site, the Chief Examiner, and the NCRA will not be held liable for any of the aforementioned mishaps that may occur. The test equipment should be marked with the test person's name and the ten digit NCRA identification number provided. Due to the stringent time frames involved, additional time will not be permitted. The test person will mark the writer disk and ASCII digit clearly with the 10-digit identification number provided by the NCRA. This number can be located on the admission ticket for the skills test. Only the test person's name and identification number is to be marked.

Test Equipment Guidelines and the Transcripts Role in the Skills Test

The test equipment guidelines mandate that whenever a CAT and writer is used without a disk, then the RAM or flash card memory must be erased. The writer's memory must be reformatted after the test. Failure to reformat the writer's memory is cause for impoundment of the writer until the following Monday Morning. The Chief Examiner has the right to impound the writer for this cause. The CAT should have the visual displays set to "Steno Notes" to prevent English translations from being shown. The transcripts are the performance record of each test person. The transcript must be created completely from scratch by the test taker. The test taker must provide his or her own CAT dictionary for the test when using CAT. The test taker is responsible for translations, editing functions, and printing procedures that are needed to create the transcript.

Guidelines That Apply to the Test Concerning the Transcript

The test taker must bring at least 20 blank sheets of white paper consisting of the minimum 20 lb. bond variety. This paper is to be used in the printers. The site may or may not provide paper, but it is best to bring an adequate supply with you to the test site. Those test takers that are using CAT shall convert their last skills test transcript files over to the ASCII format. No help can be given in this conversion of files as this is against the rules of the test. The files are to be copied onto the floppy disk to be turned into the NCRA representative present at the test site. The test takers may store the file into one total file or as three separate files. This storage is at the discretion of the test taker.

Guidelines That Apply to the Test Concerning the Transcript and Rough Drafts

The separate files given for the Literary, Jury Charge, and Testimony portions are stored as three individual computer text/transcript files. These files are to be used for editing the documents. The labeling of these files is to be given the last six digits of the examination's identification number. The six digits will end in a letter which denotes the type of file. The label will end with L for the literary files, J for the jury charge files and T for the testimony files. The skills test sections begin on a new page of the finalized hard copy version of the transcript. The rough drafts that are needed are permitted during the test. However, strict rules must be adhered to ensure the validity of the test. The pages of the rough draft will be individually labeled with the 10-digit identification number of the test.

Guidelines That Apply to the Test Concerning the Rough Draft and the Sharing of Printers

The suggestion made by the NCRA organization is to make one printed rough draft and one finalized version of the transcript. Finally, the proper disposal of the rough draft must be made prior to the test taker's departure. This disposal is witnessed by the room monitor at the time the finalized copy is handed in for grading. The test taker may share a printer with another test taker. Again, there are rules that mandate this procedure. The test taker will raise his or her hand before the initiating of any printing. The monitor must match up your identification number with the items being printed. Careful attention is given to each page's identification number to ensure that only one person is printing at a time. The monitor will check your admission ticket for verification during this process.

Guidelines Regarding the Skill Tests and Grading Criteria

Copyright laws apply to the RPR and RMR skills test. Any release or attempted release of controlled testing materials will be subject to prosecution and automatic failure. Other triggers for automatic failure include submitting a transcript that is single spaced or uses all capital or all lower-case letters, submitting a transcript in a format that cannot be printed, and continuing to work on a transcript after time has been called. Paragraphing of the transcript is recommended.

Forty-five errors are permitted on the literary RPR test. Fifty mistakes are permitted on the jury charge portion of the test. Fifty-seven mistakes are permitted on the testimony portion of the RPR exam. For the RMR, fifty errors are permitted on the literary portion of the test. Sixty errors are permitted on the RMR's jury charge portion of the test. Sixty-five mistakes are permitted on the testimony portion of the RMR test. For all tests, more than one drop of 10 or more words in a row results in automatic failure.

Common Exam Mistakes Made on the Exams

Words that have been exchanged in place of the correct word are considered wrong. Words that use the incorrect present or past tense in a sentence is considered wrong. Words that are not transcribed as singular or plural words as dictated are considered incorrect. Words that have been left out during the transcription are considered errors. Words that have been supplemented within the dictation are considered errors. Words that have been transposed within the dictation are considered errors. Each transposed word is counted as one error. Each misspelling of the word is considered one error. Transcribing the wrong name is counted as one mistake. Punctuation that has been left out or used incorrectly is counted as a mistake. Changing a word from a contraction to two words is considered one mistake. Changing two words into a contraction is considered one mistake.

Leaving off the Q and A to indicate question and answer format are considered errors. The number of counts per error depends upon the number of mistakes made in the transcription. Leaving off symbols that indicate money is a mistake. Likewise, writing the incorrect money or numeral in any transcription is counted count as a mistake. Leaving off capital letters, counts as one mistake. Corrections that have been made with a pen or pencil are wrong. Transcribing words or acronyms incorrectly can be counted as multiple errors. For example, interchanging the words United States for the abbreviation, US, can constitute two mistakes. One per each letter used incorrectly. Likewise, interchanging the abbreviation, US, for the words United States constitute as two mistakes. These typographical and grammatical errors can add up to numerous mistakes on an exam.

Arrival and Identification Process Required on the Day of the Exam

The test taker will need to provide a photo identification, admission ticket, and/or letter confirming the exam date. The test taker must allow for time for the check in and verification process. There will be a general sign-in roster for the test that is to be taken. The PES proctor will have the registration roster for the test takers taking the WKT test. The equipment that you bring to the test will need to be examined prior to admission into the test. Self-contained word processors will not be permitted at the test site without earlier authorization from the Chief Examiner. Bring a printed or electronic dictionary and possibly, a spell checker. The WKT test takers are not allowed to use any references for the exam. Test takers should observe a quiet demeanor so as not to disturb others around them.

Steps That Must Be Completed on Test Day

Test takers taking the RPR should expect to take all three portions of the skills test for one session. The RMR can be taken one portion at a time. The RPR test takers have 3 and half hours to complete the transcription. The RMR test takers have 1 and a quarter hours to complete each portion of the exam. The identification number is listed on the upper left hand corner of the test envelope. Each page of the transcript should have the exact same number listed to correspond with your examination identification number. Names will not be used. Each portion of the test will begin on a new page. Upon completion of the transcription, you should put your transcript inside the Skills Test envelope. Do not seal the envelope. The Chief Examiner or RPR/RMR Coordinator will accept the finished test.

Steps to Take If a Portion of the Test Has Not Been Completed

The steps to take if a portion of the test is not completed are simply accomplished. First, you must sign your name in the lower right hand corner of this skills test envelope. Next, you must write out the letters "NT" in the upper right hand corner of the test. The letters, "NT" stand for the words non-transcribed and indicates to the assessment personnel that the test was not completed. Finally, the test envelope is to be handed into the room's test monitor. This person is either the Chief Examiner or the RPR/ RMR coordinator present in the room. At the end of the testing period the monitor collects all test envelopes from the test takers. Failure to hand in the test envelope will result in an automatic determination of "NT". This will have a negative impact on your final score.

Aspects of the RDR Exam

Persons actively involved in consultant or leadership roles within the community and those with five years of experience as an RMR can take the Registered Diplomate Reporter Exam. The Registered Diplomate Reporter Exam can be referred to as the RDR Exam. In 1995 the NCRA organization had 236 Registered Diplomate Reporters enlisted as members. The RDR exam consists of 100 multiple-choice questions. Persons with 20 years of verified court reporting experience are eligible to take the RDR Exam. Failing that, a baccalaureate degree with at least 10 years of verified court reporting can be alternate requirements for taking the RDR Exam. Otherwise, a person with a CMRS Or a Fellow of the Academy of Professional Reporters who have also achieved a passing grade on the RMR Written Knowledge Test may take the RDR Exam. Persons who wish to receive an RDR certificate must pass the test with at least 70% or more.

Aspects of the CRR Exam

Persons who wish to take the CRR (Certified Realtime Reporter) exam should have and RPR certificate and be a member of the NCRA organization. To pass the CRR exam you must be able to set up your own equipment. You must be able to efficiently operate your equipment. You must reach speeds up to 180 to 200 wpm with accuracy for five minutes. The transcription will consist of writing in real time for five minutes from a professionally recorded straight material. You must be able to convert your file to ASCIII text file. Final submissions of text files will be graded. Persons who achieve a passing score on the CRR exam will be required to continue with their education. Education requirements consist of maintaining a minimum of 30 CE credits in five core course subjects over a three-year timeframe. Persons must also continue to hold a valid NCRA membership.

Review the Module I Training Program

In Module I, the program teaches those skills important to the role of leadership and community interaction. The program focuses on the organizational skills involving preparation and the development of a systematize plan of management. The program focuses on essentials in making good staffing decisions and in directing personnel efficiently. Decision making skills are enhanced through an examination of goal setting and problem solving methodologies. Persons are directed to become more self-aware through diagnostic survey tools. Persons work on motivation in theory and in practical applications. Leadership is discussed. Delegation and supervision are taught as part of the leadership portion of the program. Human resource management and the laws are taught. A concentration on the topics of recruitment, interview processes, hiring, and retention techniques, training for optimal efficiency, performance assessments, appropriate discipline practices, and termination of workers are discussed in detail. Team building techniques are also part of the program.

Review the Module II Training Program

In Module II, the training program teaches those skills important to the role of administration. The program focuses on standards that make for good financial management and control. The program focuses on the essentials in accomplishing the universal financial duties of all managers. Case studies are discussed in detail. Communication is stressed as an important skill for the supervisor. Education is enhanced. Reporting technology and breakouts are taught. Marketing concepts are taught. A concentration on the topics of fees, advancements, places, products, and ethical concerns are discussed in detail. The topics concerning the advertising and promotion of the reporter services are taught as part of the training program. The impact of this advertising can play a role in the management of the reporter services. This training program's objective is to increase the administrative skills of the manager to impact in a positive manner on the reporting service business.

Benefits and Requirements of Continuing Education for the Certified Reporting Instructor

The Certified Reporting Instructor's education enhances experienced court reporters that have teaching backgrounds and certification. A total of 11 hours of training will teach the following lessons: communication skills; introduction into the NCRA program and services available; proper conduct and ethics; various functions of official or freelance reporters in the court system; the legal system; the application of cognitive, affective, and psychomotor strategies as they apply to the student's learning style; development of a classroom management and style; evaluation and assessment of students within a classroom setting; standards based curricula and instructional techniques; and learning theory. The person must earn 31 continuing education credits over the next three years. Nine credits of Professional Education, nine credits of Court Reporting Education, nine credits in General Education, and three credits of electives and some CE credits are also obtained through the attendance of a NCRA promoted educational event.

Benefits and Requirements of Continuing Education for the Certified Program Evaluator

The Certified Program Evaluator's education enhances persons who have a current NCRA membership in place or for person's with RPR or CRI certification that already teach in approved NCRA programs. A total of 10 hours of training will be separated into three parts. The lessons included in Session I includes: comprehensive program on the development and understanding of interpersonal skill levels as they relate to school administrators; development of word choice skills, team interaction, and the treatment of delicate or awkward topics. The lessons included in Session II includes: program evaluation and assessment; a focus on the set up prior to the visit; responsibilities of team members; and the procedures involved with an exit interview. The lessons included in Session III includes: simulated program assessments; and learn how to assess critically your own performance.

Benefits and Requirements of Continuing Education for the Certified Legal Video Specialist

The Certified Legal Video Specialist's education enhances persons who have a desire for a fast track of one year into the industry. A total of three steps are involved in the process. First, attendance of the NCRA promoted seminar, "Videotape in the Legal Environment" is required. This is a two-day seminar with the following topics: techniques for videotaping depositions, the rules prevailing over lawful video, legal and technical jargon, and a simulated deposition in which court reporters model the use of video records used in a court setting. The lessons include: editing and playback techniques; arrangement of audio and video equipment; recordkeeping and storage systems; ethical and professional behavior; getting hold of necessary equipment; inconspicuous presence in the legal proceedings; legal video and legalities; principles used in video productions; advertising and promotional techniques.

The second step of the Certified Legal Video Specialist's seminar includes: achievement of a passing score on the CLVS Written Knowledge Test. This test is administered at same locations and times as the May and November exams given by NCRA. The third steps involve a Production test designed to demonstrate your ability to stage a mock deposition. Your score for completion of the Production Test will be based on videotape deposition guidelines and the quality of the production. Upon completion of all three certification steps, the person will have achieved the status of a Certified Legal Video Specialist. Legal video experts have a wide range of opportunities to succeed within the reporting profession as the person grows and expands in this area of expertise.

Registration Process for the NCRA Exam

Registration packets are distributed to all valid members during the first week in February for persons desiring to take the May exam. Registration packets are distributed to all valid members during the first week in August for persons desiring to take the November exam. Persons who do not receive a packet for registration purposes should call the toll-free number to request a packet. Persons are encouraged to read all the instructions before selection of the exam category. Persons are not allowed to take multiple exams. Only one test will be administered to each person registered. A choice of three test sites are indicated by the four-digit number recorded on the exam registration form. If your choice of site is not available, then a refund will be issued. Checks or money orders are accepted as payment. The forms must contain your written signature and be turned in by the deadline noted on the registration packet.

The registration process ends with a mailed confirmation letter from the NCRA organization. This letter should arrive within two weeks after the registration process has closed. The letter should include the correct exam requested and the correct site placement. The reporting time will not be listed on the confirmation letter. If a change is to be made, then make those changes on the confirmation letter. Then, mail or fax that letter with the appropriate changes back to the NCRA Testing Office by the change and withdrawal deadlines posted. Requests made after the change and withdrawal deadlines cannot be accommodated. In addition, persons who request a withdrawal due to the placement of their choice of a second or third placement test site will not be honored with a full refund. Withdrawals, but not site changes can be handled on the phone.

The fees associated with registration and refund policies. A cost of $35.00 will be applied to handle administrative costs incurred by NCRA. Partial refunds may be administered to all persons who meet the deadline criteria for such refunds. Site changes cannot be made if there is no available space at the test site to be had. Deferrals may also be called in by telephone. Otherwise, deferrals are given a onetime only option of moving the test date to the next available date. The deferral requests must be given before the deadline to qualify for a deferral status. Withdrawal deadlines for the May exam are on March 31st. Likewise, withdrawal deadlines for the November exam are for the September 30th date. Only those persons who fall ill to a serious illness or natural disaster are subject to non-forfeiture of their entire registration fee. NCRA must also be notified regarding the non-attendance.

The admission ticket for each test taker is mailed two weeks before each test date. The admission ticket will contain the following information: test site location; time of check in; name of registered test; and pertinent messages. A forfeiture of the entire test fee will be undertaken, if a person submits for a test and does not have a valid membership with NCRA. Admission tickets are not designated to persons who have not paid in full for the exam to be taken. Persons may select sites that observe the Sabbath by checking the Sabbath Observer box on their registration forms. A written letter from your clergyman authenticating your religious preference should be included. Testing accommodations will be provided in concordance with the Americans with Disabilities Act of 1990. An arrangement with the Testing Office should be conducted prior to the test date.

Receiving Test Scores

Test takers can expect to have their Skills Test graded by exam staff at the test site on the day of the exam. Those persons who achieve a score 10 points above or below the permissible number of mistakes will be rechecked by NCRA's Verification Committee. Persons may expect to receive a score through the postal system within eight weeks from the date of the test. Test takers achieving a grade of 70% or more correct answers on the WKT have passed. Test takers receiving a (P) have passed the Skills Test. Test takers receiving a (F) have failed the Skills Test. Test takers who have a (V) have had their test verified by NCRA's Verification Committee. If a person wished to receive a numerical score, then the person must submit a written request with a copy of the test results card along with payment by the deadline specified.

Recognition Certificates and the Appeal Process

A hand-lettered official certificate will be mailed to the successful test taker. Additional copies required payment along with a written request. Persons obtaining RPR and RMR certification will be recorded in the "Journal of Court Reporting" and the "Court Reporter Sourcebook". In addition, several colleges and universities will award credit hours for successful completion of the certification exam. Those persons achieving RPR certification will gain 21 credit hours. Persons achieving RMR certification will earn 3 credit hours. Any appeals should be made in written form within thirty days of the exam date. Make sure that you include full name of test taker, mail and telephone contact information, six digit NCRA identification number is listed, name of registered exam, date of exam, exam four-digit site number, and test taker's signature on all requests. NCRA will process the appeal in accordance with established NCRA criteria.

Membership with NCRA and Test History

Partial test history for persons who pass either the WKT or the Skills Test will be retained at the NCRA organization. This partial test history applies to those persons who have a valid membership with NCRA. Memberships must be renewed by January 2nd of each calendar year. A sixty-day grace period is granted, but those who have not paid by March 1st will lose credit for partial successful test scores previously achieved. A total cost of all test scores will be lost when RPR and RMR members do not pay their membership dues and do not gain the 30 continuing education credits within the three-year period. This results in the need for the persons to retake either the RPR or the RMR again. Only those persons who successfully retake and pass the exams will be awarded with certification. Again, only those persons with fully paid membership are qualified to take the exam.

Validity and Reliability of NCRA Exams

Validity implies that the test has an element of legitimacy in that it is an exam that measures or accesses what it was designed to evaluate. NCRA test takers can expect to take a test that measures their level of skill and knowledge in the subjects pertaining to court reporting. NCRA tries to maintain the validity of a test by providing: intermittent improvements of test provisions and qualifications to measure the existing knowledge and most recent practices initiated in the discipline of court reporting. Experts around the country take part in the analysis of the exam to make sure that the test meets the validity standards applied to all NCRA exams. Reliability means that the exams have been checked to make sure that each question within the test is written in such a way as to ensure that most people answer the question correctly.

Continuing Education Credits

Continuing education credits offers the person the opportunity to gain new insights and to obtain up to date information on a topic. The person can expect that the development and mastery of specific skills will be targeted. Principles of scientific and critical inquiries will be applied to build upon the foundation of good judgment necessary to perform the job of a court reporter. Persons are enriched by their educational pursuits. Education offers persons the chance to become lifelong learners that appreciate and aspire to greater educational levels. Furthermore, the authenticity of the reporter is enhanced by his efforts to gain and improve his or her education. This gives the reporter a more respectful place within the workforce. Not every state within the union requires certification from licensed reporters. NCRA's national certification offers the reporters a more reputable place within the legal community.

Classes that are evaluated as core curriculum subjects can be counted as CE credits. NCRA will accept submission forms along with a $25.00 evaluation fee to determine whether a class meets the criteria to qualify for CE credits. Grades of "C" or above on college level courses constitute as a passing grade. Only persons that receive passing grades can earn the eight credits that are administered per semester hours taken or the seven credits for earned for each trimester hour taken, or the five credits that are earned for each quarter hour of instruction. In addition, there are individual studies programs that can be taken that earn college credit that can be counted toward CE credits. These home study programs have been designed by NCRA and require a $25 fee. The home study courses are titled as follows: "The Journal of Court Reporting Articles"; "Book Review Program"; and the "Grammar for Court Reporters Test".

Credits are retained on record and reviewed at end of each three-year period. Then, a person may expect that all accumulated and unnecessary credits will be wiped away from your record. To prevent this eradication of the credits from the record a person must follow procedures set forth by the NCRA organization. Credit that has been achieved that needs to remain on record can be done so at the request of the member. Members may request a grace period of three months to keep the credits on the record. If the time extension provided by the 3-month period is not sufficient, then the only other recourse a person has is to ask for an appeal. The grace period will be deducted from the RPR term limits. These requests are made to the Continuing Education Office in timely manners.

Basic Core Curriculum Offered by NCRA

The Basic Core Curriculum offered by NCRA has five subject areas. These subject areas include: Academic Knowledge; Business Practices: Language Skills; Reporting Technology; and Electives. The registered members of NCRA are expected to earn six CE credits in all five of the subject areas. This means that the members will need a total of 30 credits over the course of a three-year period. The categories listed under Academic Knowledge include: medical, legal, technical subjects presented by experts, orientation sessions directed toward statutes, rules, procedures, and operations of a court system, real estate, cardiopulmonary resuscitation, voluntary retesting on written knowledge test at current level. The categories listed under Language Skills include: grammar, punctuation, spelling, vocabulary, etymology, sentence structure, paragraphing, proofreading, usage, contribution of other languages to English, Regional and minority dialects, colloquialisms, commonly heard slang, literature, journalism and or composition, foreign languages, and semantics.

The categories listed under Business Practices include: Statutes and regulations, management, ethics knowledge and application of NCRA Code of Professional Ethics, Marketing, Public relations, substance abuse, and health. The categories listed under Reporting Technology include shorthand/machine skills, CAT skills, Shorthand writing and editing skills, General requirements and responsibilities of reporters, emerging technologies, research, computer hardware, and computer software. The electives will consist of any CE credit under the four categories already listed. Seminars that are approved by NCRA may earn CE credits. Tests of speed must qualify as RMR levels to qualify a person to receive CE credits. Speed contests for each NCRA leg counts toward 5 CE technology credits. State speed contests or Award of Excellence contests counts towards 4 CE technology credits. Mentors of interns will receive CE Academic credits.

Home Study Course Content

One home study course is titled, "The Journal of Court Reporting Articles". This study has two or three page articles followed by brief multiple-choice quizzes. Persons who receive 75% on the tests are marked with a passing score. Persons will receive credit for each test passed on a one time only basis. A test can only be counted once for credit. The Book Review Program has a 20-question test for each of the 50 books listed in the program. Three credits will be given for a passing test of score of any 85%. The "Grammar for Court Reporters Test" is taken in two parts. Part one has 80 questions, part two has hundred questions. The persons receiving a score of 70% or more earn 3 credits. These tests will not be administered for credit to the same person more than once every five years.

Achieving Passing Scores on the NCRA Tests

The best practices before a test call for methods that will increase the retention of learning. Some suggestions to accomplish retention are to repeat the information over and over in a variety of ways. First, write the information on a note card. Next, read the information aloud. Finally, listen to the information on tape. Keep the information to be reviewed nearby throughout the day. Then review terminology and information that will be on the test intermittently throughout the day. An expectation of what will be on the test includes multiple choice items, fill in the blank questions, matching items, and true or false questions. Then, review each section of like categories so that you can more thoroughly comprehend and review a subject. Do not write your answers in your resource materials for the tests.

Speed Stroke Errors

Believe in yourself and you will be able to make positive changes in your learning. Practice until you have accomplished just the right skill. Real-time reporting requires accuracy and elimination of hesitations in typing with speed. Faltering execution of speed strokes can negatively impact skill levels. Hesitations in strokes can cause errors that slow down speeds. The certain, sure strokes that are practiced should remove errors. Persons should practice listening to copy and hand typing. There are three reasons why you may have problems with drops or mis-strokes in your typing. One reason includes hesitations due to theory problems having to do with the vowel sounds, initial or final consonant combinations, or other phonetically related reasons. The second reason is due to the briefs and/phrases that are not habitual in our movements. Additionally, some fingering combinations are mechanically clumsy to produce.

When you practice, you need to deliberate on the two areas in which you find yourself making the mistakes. First, begin practicing your speed from pre-recorded tapes at just below your speed level. Never try to force accuracy and control, instead work at just below your present speed. Look over your notes to determine the areas in which your hesitations occur. Then, practice and stretch your speed listening to hear the sounds that are just outside your comfort zone. Remember to work as accurately as possible. Speed is important, but only in conjunction with maintaining accurate strokes. Printed materials like books or magazines are good practice tools. When you notice the places that you had to think about how to write a word or a place where you obviously had a hesitation, then you should re-create the position of your fingers. Analyze for proper technique and improvements.

Ways to Increase Speed and Omit Errors

Pay attention to the positioning of your fingers so that you can correct techniques and improve your speeds. Then, daily practice proper finger drill positions. Next, look at theory practice on specific problem principles. Finally, work on phrase practices to alleviate specific drawbacks. Work on word lists and on complete sentences where the specific improvements should be applied. Speeds can be increased as a person becomes more comfortable and more refined in moving their fingers across the keypad. Reporters should be able to move their fingers from any position on the steno keypad, the target outline, and to other keyboard positions to create the desired phrase with accuracy. The likelihood of the person committing the same errors over and over is lessened as the person's skill level increases. The key to improvement involves the willingness to analyze the mistake, to compensate for the mistake, and to practice the correct techniques.

Successful Approaches to Taking the Test

Some success has been made in visualization. Visualize yourself taking the test. Put yourself there in your mind and then, tell yourself that you can pass the test. Do not allow yourself talk to be negative or defeating. Instead, be persistent even if you run across an obstacle. Keep trying until you accomplish your goals. Take on every opportunity to stretch and strengthen your skills. Do not allow yourself the luxury of procrastination. Make the time to strengthen your performance levels. On the day of the test, allow your attitude to be one in which you believe in yourself. With a single-minded determination, you should focus and concentrate on the task at hand. Concentration is a skill. All skills can be learned and practiced until flawless results occur. It is advisable to filter out extraneous noise and report proceedings verbatim.

Increasing Concentration

Activities of the human brain can increase concentration. No other computer can work like the brain to filter out extraneous sounds and focus entirely on relevant events. Practice your mental skills to increase your powers of concentration. Close your eyes a few minutes to increase your attention to the sounds in the room. Then, begin work with a renewed sense of intensity and concentration. Practice your skills in ignoring sounds in your surroundings that are inconsequential. Practice in conditions that are less than perfect to desensitize yourself to distractions. On test day, do not let yourself to be distracted by the activities of others. Do not pay attention to background noises and activities, but focus only on your writing speed and accuracy. If you miss a word or make a mistake, then stay calm. Remember, you have prepared and are a competent reporter.

Increasing Relaxation and Confidence

You must cultivate a method by which you can personally keep in check your attention skills to specifically concentrate on the task at hand. If you have a personal interest in the subject matter, then research has shown that you will be better equipped to focus your attention while learning. Likewise, research has shown that more effort is required to focus on topics you have no interest. Boredom can make the learning process slow and tedious. A break from the learning situation can provide a respite that increases the person's attention and concentration upon their return to the task. The following strategies can assist you in increasing your relaxation during a learning process. 1. Avoid disruptions as much as possible. 2. Make yourself comfortable in your learning environment. 3. Work in a quiet place where you can avoid visual and audible distractions. 4. Manage your thought processes to avoid distractions.

Advantages of a Person vs. a Recording Device in Documenting the Proceedings

The certified shorthand reporter has a definite advantage over the audio or video tape recordings done during live court reporters. The video and audio tape recordings can be useless if the tapes do not have a corresponding audio track and audio recordings that has the capabilities of discriminating relevant sounds from extraneous sounds that are heard in the court room. Typically, audio recordings result in an incomprehensible jumble of blurred voices and extraneous noises. Only persons trained to distinguish the sounds can transcribe the tape-recordings with accuracy. Once you have given your attention over to learning and mastering the theory of court reporting you may refocus your efforts on developing the skills of accuracy and speed. With much practice and experience a person will be able to perfectly relate what is heard to the fingertips for transcription purposes.

Building Your Concentration During Your Transcription

A positive mental state is part of the practice session. As the dictation is being read the role of relaxation can be an asset in concentrating. Gaining relaxation skills does involve the controlling of emotions. Anxious feelings from boredom or worry can create distractions in the workplace. A mind set of impartiality can allow you to detach yourself from uneasiness, fears, or distresses which divert you from your work. Some techniques include imagining yourself in a happy, peaceful environment. The payback of achieving relaxation and concentration skills will add to your ability as a court reporter. As you become more confident in basic physical actions of a reporter on a daily basis, then those areas where you required the most concentrative efforts will no longer requiring such intense concentration efforts. This will allow you to improve and to renew your efforts of concentration to new skills and more difficult matters.

Increasing Transcription Speeds

Use good quality tapes for transcription practice. Professionally recorded tapes are available from NCRA's catalog. Use tapes of a moderate difficulty level for building speed. Use the practice tapes in conjunction with methods that will allow you to increase your speed levels and accuracy. Practicing short segments will allow you to build speed. One example would be that a person that types at a speed of 160 wpm should practice short segments at increments of 150, 160 wpm, and 170 wpm, then returning to 160 wpm. This is not an instantaneous process, but rather a fast track to increase overall speed skills. Improvements at one level should be made in regards to accuracy before you go on to next level of speed. Use tapes within a range of only 10 to 20 wpm of your speed capabilities now. Then, develop your accuracy levels before advancing to the next level.

Reading back is essential in your speed building practice. Small errors can account for big errors in a court setting. The difference between the words, "a" and "I" cab be truly significant in the writing of a verbatim record. You should analyze your read back records to eliminate these types of errors from your writing. Keep a record of words that were either novel to you or brought about a hesitation in your transcription. Practice these words to help increase your accuracy and speed skills. If you are typing and realize that you have made a mistake, try not to let it fluster you. First you need to stay in control whenever a drop occurs. Do not try to back track in your work. Rather, minimize the number lost words by continuing in your work. Refocus your efforts on the words being spoken and allow your fingers to remain on task.

Speed Building Troubleshooting Methods

There are key areas that should be addressed for speed building. The first area involves efficient, quick movements during the physical act of typing. It is highly recommended that you have thoroughly memorized the keyboard location for each letter, number, and symbol. Next, you should be familiar with the shortened forms, abbreviations, and theories associated with writing a word the most efficiently. You should make sure that you have a comprehensive speaking, reading, writing, and shorthand vocabulary. Shorthand vocabularies must be performed without hesitations. You should be thoroughly aware of how to record responses without thinking about whether it is a phrase or an abbreviation. Additionally, you should not need to think about the spelling or the definition of a word. Nor, should you waste time trying to figure out what word the speaker pronounced. You should not mouth the words silently.

There are additional areas that should be addressed for speed building efficiency. You should not repeat the words to yourself while you are typing. You should not have to paraphrase a section because you have not the acquired skills that are essential for the creation of a verbatim report. Do not second guess your work. Do not change your work once it has been recorded. Do not substitute words that have not been dictated. Do not omit the correct punctuation as this may change the meaning or content of the writing. Arrive early enough to organize your space and to gain comfortable control over your space. Do practice constant breathing techniques, positive facial expressions, good posture, and relaxation of muscles, listening techniques, and mental attitude to gain an advantage over nerve-racking circumstances in the workplace. Use these calming techniques daily until they become automatic responses to stress.

Increasing Speed and Accuracy When Transcribing Straight Copy

Straight copy refers to hard copy or printed materials. You should use printed materials to copy to shorthand formats. This will allow you to have ample sources of practice materials as materials are readily available. Sources of printed material include: newspapers, periodicals, and textbooks. Straight copy practice can be individualized to fit your needs. You can have increased accessibility to this type of speed building methodology as it is one that can be done from any location. You can use this method with other persons. You learn to read back your notes to others. You may employ the services of a relative, a friend, or fellow student as you practice. You can readily see the improvements made each time you practice. You can also change your routine in a variety of ways. You learn to think in "machine shorthand". You can become proficient at evaluation and correction of your own work.

Practicing Straight Copy

Begin with materials that have proper names, new terminology and up to date events. Using the same source each day allows you the opportunity of working at a more even level of density. Make a list of preview words from the selected material. The preview list should have words with difficult strokes and outlines, proper names, words in other languages; small words that are used incorrect often; unfamiliar outlines; words that need to be defined or need to be known, words that are difficult to pronounce; arbitraries, expressions, and brief forms. Do not preview all the words in the section of selected material as this makes the exercise useless for your needs. Use the preview list in this manner: write words 10-15 times each; read back shorthand each time you write the selection; remember to write until you have achieved rhythm and eliminated all hesitations.

Straight copy should be a timed practice. A good time limit is for three minutes for each session. Again, time your read back practice for the same three-minute session. Identified hesitations or mis-strokes should be words added to the preview list. Use punctuation in your practice sections. Set speed goals to ensure that you are improving. Practice should be daily for a set period. One suggested period includes an hour a day of practice. Keep a journal of the amount of words you practice daily and your speeds. This practice of logging your hours and improvement can be a great encouragement as you can see your progression in the logs. You can better judge the days that you will perform efficiently. Repeat the steps: preview, train using the preview list, write article, establish goals, write from printed copy, read back shorthand, go over each step, and log improvements daily.

Value of Proper Listening Techniques and Repetition

Court reporters must remain focused on the speaker. A good technique for remaining focused on the listener begins with the act of continuing writing despite mistakes. Another technique involves a focal point. Select a focal point that keeps your eyes from moving about the room. Move on to another object as a focal point as the first object loses interest. Finally, maintain your listening by focusing intently on the speaker. Keep at bay any stray thoughts. You must practice diligently to develop good listening techniques if you hope to be a good court reporter. Apply the 3 listening techniques at every opportunity to gain proper listening techniques and to achieve better test results. Repetitious practice allows you to rework difficult spots to the point that they no longer hinder you. Remember mis-strokes will not go away until your technique has been perfected by replacing the wrong action with the corrected fingering techniques.

Frequent Words

The 100 words: the, of, and, to , a, in , that, is, was, he, for, it, with, as, his, on, be, at, by, I, this, had, not, are, but, from, or, have, an, they, which, one, were, you, her, all, she, there, would, we, their, him, been, has, when, who, will, more, no, if, out, so, said, what, up, its, about, into, than, them, can, only, other, new, some, could, time, these, two, may, then, do, first, any, my, now, such, like, our, over, man, me, even, most, made, after, also, did, many, before, must, through, back, year, where, much, your, way, well, down. These words should be practiced in sets of three to do away with any hesitations or faltering between words. Practice the words as they appear in a sentence to ensure accuracy in your writing efforts.

Using Audio Books in Practice

Audio books can be found in the library, rental stores, or in book stores. Libraries offer an inexpensive source for this practice media. Books can be selected on your preference of entertainment selections. The three areas that should be included in the audio practice include: theory development, a variety of dictation materials, and an assortment of speed building strategies. Theory development involves the making of outlines and theory patterns used in writing your practice sections. The concepts that strengthen this development include the creation of conflict free outlines, the use of computer-aided transcriptions, and the read back methodology applied. New material is useful in developing accuracy in your writing. Old material is useful in building up speeds in your writing. One speed building exercise includes two minutes of transcription of the material beginning at the control speed and working up towards ever increasing speeds ending with a return to the control speed.

Additional Methods for Increasing Skills

One method for increasing skills using audio books as practice includes maintaining a transcription for a period of five minutes. This method gains the increase of endurance. Persons should practice until they can take down dictation for sustained periods. You may need to have a friend dictate a practice session for you. This session can be recorded on audio tapes. Make it a habit to practice at a designated time each day. Practice every day of the week. Give yourself a set goal to accomplish for the day. Give yourself a break between sessions. Each session should include practice times on theory, speed building, and reading back dictation. Use self-assessment techniques to target problem areas in your writing. Each practice session should be approached with an attitude of positive thinking. Drills should focus on word combinations, controlling speeds, and on individual needs.

S. Sanford Heller has developed finger exercises designed to increase speeds. The ring finger and the pinkie finger are the fingers that normally slow progress. These fingers are the ones that appear the weakest for hand motions. A good way to practice the strengthening of these fingers for the right hand includes the following drills: EGT: ELS UGT: ELS EGT: ULS UGD: ELZ EGD: ELZEGD: ULZ EKT: EMS UKT: EMS UMZ: EKD UKD: EMZ EKT: UMS IGT:ILS IGT:ULS UGT:ULS EGT:ULS UGT:ILS EGT:ILS A good way to practice the strengthening of these fingers for the left hand includes the following drills: KHA:DWO KHO:DWO SMO:DWO SMA:DWO KHA:FWO KMO:STRA KMA:STRO JA:DPO JO:DPA KHO:FWA JO:FLA JA:FLO SHAO:DO SHO:DAO You need control and flexibility to increase your speeds. Control allows you to place your fingers where you intend them to be quickly. Flexibility allows you the manual dexterity to move your fingers to perform the required strokes.

Time Management

Time management involves planning. Planning should begin with the recording of your activities on a calendar or weekly/daily planner. Incorporate some time for preferred or choices of activities. Use your schedule as a tool to give you some flexibility and fun in your day. Pinpoint the activities which cause you pleasure or stress. Likewise, pinpoint the activities which are productive and non-productive to meeting your ultimate goals. Eliminate those that are not important to your over-all plan. Do not waste time in handling papers more than once. Make a decision about the paperwork and handle it accordingly. Log everything that you do to better target the areas of time that you are unproductive. Do not overbook your schedule. In times of heavy stress and overbooking, allow yourself the ability to cancel items that are not priorities. Do not let others have control over your schedule to the point where you no longer manage your time efficiently.

STRESS

Stress can have some negative effects on your health. Stress has been linked to ulcers, heart attacks, phlebitis, Crohn's disease, colitis, and other health concerns. Too much sugar, fat, salt, or peanut butter in the diet can lead to poor health. Proteins, fruits, and vegetables are a healthier alternative. Preferred activities should be included into your schedule three to four times a week. These preferred activities should be noncompetitive, not involve fault finding opportunities, personally rewarding, accomplished as an individual, and less taxing mentally. Some suggestions in areas that can be selected for your preferred activities include: walking, hobbies, fishing, hunting, reading, gardening, cooking, house cleaning, weight lifting, musical interludes, journal writing, praying, spiritual endeavors, shopping, television viewing, socializing, or other activities that promote feelings of enjoyment. One resource includes the book, "Court Reporters and Stress: How to Find Time to Live" by Dr. Barbara Barnett. This book is available on cassette.

VISUALIZING COURT REPORTING GOALS

Goals are accomplished when you can see yourself performing the result successfully. A motivational collage can help you accomplish the first visualization exercise. Begin your visualization by listing 7 goals that you wish to accomplish. Then, say the goals aloud to yourself seven times each morning. Reflect on these goals throughout the day. Repeat this act of positive self-talk for 21 days. Then, on the 22nd day, you are ready to begin a new list. A motivational collage is a gathering of clippings of magazines that symbolizes or inspires an image concerning your individual objectives. For instance, if you plan to go on taking a trip, you might want to clip out a picture of the place you intend to visit. This can also be used as a study tool. Paste pictures on a collage to help you remember key points.

ACHIEVING THE RPR, RMR, OR SPEED CONTEST CERTIFICATES

Do not expect to pass the test without practice. Practice is an essential part of building speed up and defeating nerves that can inhibit your progress. Do not practice on the day of the test. It is best to practice an hour a day for weeks than to try to cram practice sessions into a few days. You do not want to tire yourself out before a test. You should also make sure that you can read your transcription with accuracy. Compare your notes stroke for stoke to determine that there are no mis strokes to lessen the errors that have the potential to cause you to fail the test. Use a rule or straightedge to keep your place on your notes. Do not use your creative writing skills to substitute for ineligible strokes. Use AE in your notes after a phrase to differentiate between a contraction and two words.

PREPARATION FOR PASSING THE RPR EXAM

You should lay out all your supplies and carefully pack them the night before the test. Pack equipment in a luggage carrier for transport. Double check the folds of the steno paper. Equipment should be checked to ensure that adequate power supplies are available; test typewriter and word processing ribbons and make sure they are in working order. A good night's sleep is highly advised. Eat a proper light, meal before test time. Avoid sugar and caffeine products. Take a short walk around the test site before the test. Arrive on time and get your belongings organized. Dress in comfortable, loose fitting garments in layers. The layers allow you to adjust your clothing to fit the room's temperature. Warm up your fingers with simple, familiar exercises or drills for a few minutes. Use paperclips to mark your notes for later reference.

Highlight folds and then check that a note has continuity and no lines have been omitted. Keep your mind on your own preparations. Keep an optimistic point of view. Practice mental conditioning techniques to keep anxious thoughts at bay. Do not allow your thought process to distract you from the task at hand. Keep a good sense of humor about you. Think of a goal that you have already achieved with a high degree of success. Encourage yourself with this thought. Select a focal point for the dictation process. Keep transcribing at the speed that the reader is dictating. Transcribe one syllable at a time. Do not let your mind fill in the blanks from the story being told. Figure out problem syllables by the sounds that they make, not by filling in the blanks. Trust that your notes are correct representations of the dictated material. Do not try to second guess your notes.

Ten Positive Ways to Impact Your Test Taking

Test taking begins in the preparation of the test. First, register as a member of NCRA. Then, submit your registration packet for the exam before the deadline. The registration packet should be prepared per the instructions. Submit the packet along with an $85.00 fee for registration. The registration should be sent to the correct address that is listed on the registration packet envelope. Reading of the registration booklet will allow you to be completely informed about important aspects of the test. Keep this booklet for future reference. Upon receipt of the NCRA acknowledgement card, you should review your instructions. On the day of the test, you should report in a timely manner and carry your admission ticket. This ticket will be needed for admission into the exam. Remember to bring the specified identification for check in procedures.

Court Reporter Ethics

Origination of Ethics

The origination of ethics has been traced back to the days of Aristotle and Socrates. This earlier focus on ethics was deemed important in terms of morality and virtuosity. Ethics is a word derived from the Greek word signifying "character". Aristotle believed that persons do the right things out of habit. However, he also believed that people could train themselves to do the right things. In the 18th and 19th centuries, the Teleological Ethical theory was fostered. This was a theory that allowed that the result of an action can be used to determine the rightness of an action. Deontological Ethics was designed as a response to the Teleological Ethical theory. The internal characteristic of good will was the basis of this moral law or categorical imperative. This allowed that the person would perform in accordance to his internal good will despite any circumstance.

Role of Ethics in Court Reporting

Ethics in the legal community has been given a broad definition. However, there are some guiding concerns that a reporter should remain circumspect about. These concerns include the legality of an action and fairness issues. One might consider whether the action is met with a sense of fair play for all members concerned. Likewise, you might want to consider how the action makes you feel. Persons may want to ensure that their actions promote a sense of pride to themselves and to those within their community. You might want to review applicable statutes within your geographic area to further ensure that you follow ethical guidelines. A review of local custom and practices may be warranted. Seek advice from veteran reporters in new or complicated circumstances. Excuse yourself from private conversations between clients and counsels when opposing sides of counsel are not present.

Purchasing of Transcripts

If you are questioned concerning a private discussion among client and counsel, then reply as a deposition officer. This position insists upon one of neutrality and impartiality. Do not be afraid of reminding counsel of that position. You should not share your opinions or judgments concerning a case or witness. Whenever you offer a service to one side of counsel, you must offer this same service to the opposing side. Your ethical responsibility is to offer equality of service to both sides of counsel. This offer does not have a time limitation. Deposition testimony is not subject to the same laws of public record unless and until the original deposition transcript has been filed or lodged with the court. This means that 90 % or more of all deposition testimony should not be produced as public record. Only actual parties to the lawsuit or representative counsel should be given lee way to purchase transcripts.

Juvenile proceedings are not held in open court. Therefore, they are not subject to public record. Only the court, district attorney, the juvenile, the juvenile's parents or guardians, or representative counsel are permitted to purchase the transcripts. Cases that are considered as "in camera" proceedings are those in which are reported only in the judge's chambers. The persons usually present for these hearings include the judge, the court reporter, the defendant, and the defense counsel. These hearings cannot be given or discussed with the district attorney. This action will result in a mistrial. These hearings are sealed in a separate transcript volume in an envelope and designated by case title, date, place, and type of proceedings held. The clerk of court will take possession of the envelope and dispense appropriately. "In camera" rulings given out later by the judge during open court sessions are given the same consideration by the court reporter.

Sensitive Issues

Some sensitive issues involve protective provisions. Testimonies can receive a protective order provision that receives the marking of "confidential for counsel's eyes only". These types of marking ensure that the envelope is sealed and that the confidential deposition is treated appropriately. The testimony is sealed before being given to the counsel for review. Any testimony considered not be confidential is not sealed in this manner. You may seek clarification by questioning the attorney if you are unsure whether testimony should be marked in this manner. Maintaining the air of neutrality and impartiality is all a part of the role that a court reporter must play in the proceedings. Common sense and good judgment must be applied in this area as each situation may require separate actions. However, a good court reporter will allow these guidelines to support the profession in an ethical manner.

Preamble and the Code of Professional Ethics

In 1985, the Committee on Professional Responsibility was formed to replace the Committee on Ethics. In 1979, the Code of Professional Responsibility, Enforcement and Disciplinary Procedures, and Professional Practice Objectives were presented. This was later changed and amended with the Mediation Procedures for the Membership. The Mediation Procedures for the membership established a more harmonious way to settle disputes. The title of the Enforcement and Disciplinary Procedures was changed to Complaint Procedures. In 1992 these changes were confirmed and adopted. The extension of the Guidelines for Professional Practice, Sections I, II, and III were initiated in 1994. The sections were broken down as follows: Section I allowed for the reporter guidelines in making the official record; Section II allowed for the real-time reporter's role in legal proceedings; and Section III allowed for the real-time educational reporter course of actions to be regulated.

Persons wishing to learn more about the ethical relationship between the NCRA member and the legal community should consult the Code of Professional Ethics. These codes are designed to help the member to use good ethical values when working as a court reporter. Guidelines have been published with the mandated expectations for behavior. The Guidelines for Professional Practice includes a guideline which provides a solid framework for the operating practices of a reporter. These guidelines are not comprehensive examples of every possible scenario. Rather, these guidelines are to provide the reporter with a jumping off point to help them in their effort in maintaining the highest standard of ethical behavior. Persons unsure of ethical or moral implications should carefully consult the Code of Professional Ethics and the Guidelines for Professional Practice. Compliance with these recommended expected behaviors can result in a more professional demeanor in the workplace.

Regulations to Follow

Members should relate to all other constituents with a good measure of fairness and impartiality. Members should take special precautions to avoid situations that may be regarded as conflicts of interest. Whenever these sensitive situations arise the member should make every effort possible to clear up any hint of impropriety. The member shall reveal the point of conflict to avoid awkward situations. Reporters must be above all hint of impropriety by keeping themselves away from the situations that can damage their reputations or impugned their character. Secure verbal and written information will be held with the utmost confidentiality in accordance with the law. The member shall make no misrepresentation of his or her qualifications or services. Public statements will only be made with accuracy. Freelance reporting behaviors are not to influence the official duties and responsibility of the reporter.

The member should abide by lawful agreements regarding fees and payments. Occasionally, a court or statute may apply established fees that set the amount that a reporter may charge for a service. Reporters should avoid any unlawful agreements or contracts with other professionals. Reporters are not allowed to receive gift or incentives that range in amounts of over $100.00 in value over the course of one year. The reporter should not take any direct or indirect gifts or incentives from lawyers, clients, witnesses, insurance companies, or anyone within the legal community involved with a legal proceeding. The member should uphold the honor of the reporting community. The member must follow the Bylaws and the NCRA Constitutional Laws. The member will find that conduct becoming to a NCRA member will be one that gives the person a respectful place within the reporting profession.

Guidelines of Section I

Court reporters should only accept assignments that can be accomplished with competency and accuracy. The reporters' skills must be such that they can prepare an accurate transcript for the proceedings being held. If a reporter finds that he or she does not have the ability to complete the assignment, then the reporter should request that the assignment be given to another more qualified reporter. The reporter should set up the record in accordance with the transcription's preparation guidelines. These guidelines have been established by the NCRA or by statute, or court order. If a reporter must enlist the services of a substitute reporter, then, that reporter is responsible to notify the parties engaging the member for those duties. The substitute reporter must be one that can assume the responsibilities of the member.

The reporter is responsible for proper storage of the shorthand notes taken during a proceeding. These notes must remain in storage for a period of no less than five years. The notes must remain in their original state as hardcopy notes or electronic notes. Notes may be formatted as computer disks, cassettes, backup tape systems, or optical, or laser disk systems. Reporters are responsible for the delivery of the transcripts on the promised date of delivery. However, the reporter must assume that the timeliness of a transcript is expected even if no promised date of delivery is given. The reporter must continue to improve and perform the skills associated with the task of a professional. The reporter is responsible for remaining up to date on current literature, technological advances and developments, and to actively seek skills through continuing education programs.

The reporter should take active part in national, state, and local associations and their events. These events will allow the reporter to stretch his or her abilities and to meet the standards set forth by the reporting profession. The reporter must work as a team with the legal association and to advance the administration of the justice system. The reporter must work with qualified legal assistance organization to offer free legal services to the indigent populations. This service is a necessary part of the shorthand reporting professions' commitment to the principle that reporting services should be presented to all people despite their ability to pay. The reporter has a duty in this area to maintain the highest degree of professionalism. In addition, those duties should correspond to the professional commitments of the reporter maintaining neutrality, proficiency, and honor.

Guidelines of Section II

The duties of a real-time reporter include the provision of on-screen translation during the proceeding as it occurs. This is a needed service for the deaf populations. Persons who are deaf may need to be a part of the proceedings as the defendant, the plaintiff, the juror, or the witnesses. The real-time reporter is not present during the proceeding to provide the verbatim record. Instead, the real-time reporter may need to have his or her position clarified. The real-time reporter is to use the real-time skills and equipment for providing translation for persons who have disabilities. The real-time reporter with assistive technology should clarify the following: the person who has hired his or her services; the material that needs to be reported; the use of real-time as assistive technology and/or as a verbatim record.

It is possible that the reporter may need to provide both assistive technology and a verbatim record. However, this must be clarified in the beginning of the proceeding. In addition, the ownership of the residual computer note file must be established prior to the proceedings. The accessibility, sales, and distribution of the documents must be established. The names of those who shall have accessibility for the distribution must be clearly stated in each case. This prevents any misunderstandings later. The reporter must keep all the information related to the proceeding and the case under strict confidence. The reporter must provide as close as possible the verbatim translation for real-time assistive technology purposes, even if a verbatim record is not needed. The reporter is responsible to deliver the content of the message being uttered.

A computer translatable version accomplishes this delivery. Parentheticals are used in the document to describe sounds uttered that are not able to be translated into words. This gives the non-hearing person a better understanding of possible distractions or moods within the court. The reporter must refrain from making personal comments. The reporter must refrain from giving advice. The reporter shall only accept those assignments for which she or he is qualified to perform. The reporter must look to the setting of a situation and the clients to determine if they possess the skills that will be needed to do the job of real-time reporting in each case. The reporter should have mastered the software and hardware systems used for real-time reporting.

The reporter should be able to perform simple trouble-shooting tasks in an efficient manner. The reporter should continue to gain skills through active participation in workshops, professional conferences, and through seeking advice from other professionals in the field. The professional should be well read on subjects relating to the position of real-time reporting. The reporter will have real-time certifications on state and national levels. The reporter will need to save the actual translation disk as presented to the deaf party. This disk should contain the unedited information that was exhibited on the screen during the proceedings. The job definitions may be inserted later if the translation is not changed in any way. There are questions concerning the veracity of presenting a record that is not truly verbatim.

There are concerns about changing testimonies and about the possibility of unduly influencing the jury with a presentation of a less than verbatim record. There are also questions about the conduct of a real-time reporter during jury deliberations. The questions involve whether the jury deliberations should be included as a formal record. Jury deliberations are not normally prone to documentation. There are questions as to whether a deaf juror should receive a rough draft of the transcript and if that record should be permitted in the jury room. For hearing juror members, this is not a privilege allowed. Hearing Jury members may request for 'read backs' if they need to hear the material again. There are valid questions that have yet to be fully addressed due to the complexity and the laws associated with individuals with disabilities.

Guidelines of Section III

The Real-time Educational Reporter is a reporter that has been designates a group of one or more students for a session of classes. This reporter goes to class along with his or her designated students. The Real-time reporter serves the needs of the student in providing a real-time translation. The student can expect to receive a real-time translation based on the oral lesson given by the teacher of the class. The text of the lecture is displayed on a computer monitor for ease of access by the student that is hard of hearing or deaf. When the class ends, the reporter gives the student a copy of real-time translation of the lesson. The translation copy may be in the format of an unedited ASCII file on disk or in an edited printed form.

The Real-time Educational Reporter should coordinate with the classroom instructor to ensure that technical technology is defined before the lecture. The reporter can then enter that information into the computer's dictionary so that the reporter can translate the lectured material at a high rate of speed. The reporter should handle this position with confidentiality. Assignments are not to be shared with others. The reporter should maintain his or her role as communication facilitator. The reporter should not give advice or participate with the class in any manner. The reporter may facilitate the communication process by translating in real-time the discussions between the student, instructor, and members of the class. The reporter is responsible for setting up the equipment needed. The set up should be such that the computer screen and the speaker are visible to the student at all times.

The translation and text display are exhibited seconds after the words have been typed. The instructor should make the appropriate accommodations for the student by allowing enough time for the student to answer. Another accommodation that should be made is the restriction of class dialogues to one speaker at a time. The reporter's responsibilities include a like representation of verbatim translation as possible. This representation should convey the message of the speaker in content with expressions. Occasionally, words will not be translated exactly and can be substituted for words recognized by the computer translator so that the student gains understanding of the word being expressed. Sounds within the classroom must be translated. The speaker should be identified in the translation. For instance, when the instructor is speaking, the reporter would write the word instructor and a colon before the statement spoken by the instructor.

Sounds within the classroom would be indicated by surrounding the word to indicate the sound with parenthesis. If there is laughter in the room, it should be indicated in the text by this symbol (laughter). This is just one of many sounds that may need to be recorded within the text. The student would need to write down any written materials that are given on the board, in a slide show presentation, or given in another written format. The reporter is not responsible for this material. The reporter should only take on this responsibility when his or her skill levels are adequate to perform the duties of a Real-time Educational Reporter. The reporter must maintain a good working relationship with the teacher, the student, and the other class members. The reporter is responsible to obtain the services of a substitute if an absence is necessary.

Guidelines of Section IV

There are times that court reporters provide uncertified rough draft transcripts to parties involved in litigation. These rough draft transcripts are addressed under the National Court Reporters Associations suggested guidelines. It is suggested that the reporter take measures to determine appropriate conduct that is required in relation to the legal and civic community. The reporter has the responsibility to maintain a role in which does not impede the administration of justice. Laws, rules, and court orders should be applied when warranted. A reporter should maintain constant professionalism and gain the necessary skill levels that are required. The reporter should uphold a state of impartiality, good judgment, and fairness. Comparable services should be offered to all parties involved to ensure that a state of impartiality has been maintained. Uncertified rough draft transcripts should be clearly marked with the words, "computer uncertified rough draft transcript only".

Only certified transcripts should have the following items included: title page, appearance page, certificate page, the swearing in of the witness, footers with firm names or reporter names, CSR number, index page, line numbers, borders around the text, or time sampling. Uncertified transcripts should not have any of the items included under certified transcripts included in the document. In fact, the clear markings of "computer uncertified rough draft transcript" should be listed on the header, and the footer of each page. These words are also listed within the text at intermittent intervals. The uncertified copy is produced on colored paper for further distinction. A hand stamp with the phrase, "Uncertified rough draft transcript" shall be marked on each page of the document. A computer diskette copy should be distinctly marked with the same phrase with a distinctive color of ink.

Distinctive coloring ensures that the uncertified copy differs from the certified copy's page colors. The uncertified copy will be issued in a condensed format with no absolute line numbers. The uncertified transcript should have a disclaimer and an order form inserted in the cover sheet of the document. The disclaimer keeps parts of the script from being used without permission from the court. The court reporter should maintain accurate records of the disclaimer and order form requests for future reference. The reporter should not distribute an uncertified transcript with untranslated steno strokes or conflicts. Unedited transcripts with errors of more than 1% should not be distributed. The court reporter should be able to provide readable transcripts before attempting the task of presenting an uncertified rough draft transcript. The court reporter should be able to produce conflict writing using software with automatic conflict capabilities.

The court reporter should be able to use speaker identification markings within the text of the translation. The court reporter should be able to produce translations that have rates of 1% or less of untranslatable material. The court reporter should be able to use appropriate punctuation with accuracy. The suggestions made are not meant to discourage the reporter. However, it is recommended that the suggestions be applied to correct untranslates within the material. Down times can be used to make the necessary corrections to the documents. This will ensure that your work is of good quality before submission to counsel. A rough draft ASCII disk or printed transcript should be of good quality and meet the standards suggested upon presentation to counsel. These suggested standards were agreed upon by the NCRA Board of Directors on March 10, 1996.

Complaint Procedures Under the Code of Professional Ethics (Code) and the Constitution and Bylaws (C&B)

The filing and investigation of complaints are accomplished through the procedures laid out by the NCRA. The Executive Director of the Association only accepts written complaints that have been signed by the person with the complaint. These documents should include the following; name and address of the Member complaint is against; a thorough description of the conduct being questioned; references listing the provisional codes and/or the C&B regulations that are in violation; a verified affidavit with affirmation the statements made are valid. The verified affidavit must include: complainant's authorization of the Association to disclose the contents of the complaint to the parties involved. The parties involved include the Member in question; the members of the Committee on Professional Ethics, the Association Directors, the officers on staff, and if warranted, the public community.

In some instances, the public will need to be informed. The public is only informed when actual censure, suspension or expulsion of a Member is required. The public is informed through the publication of the Member's name in the Association's Journal of Court Reporting. The Executive Director will notify the Member making the complaint that the complaint has been received. The Director will also distribute copies of the complaint procedures to the complainant. The complainant will be advised to furnish any missing information. The complainant can expect that no action will be taken when information has not been furnished as requested. Once the information has been obtained, the Director will furnish the information to the Member in question.

The Member in question will receive a copy of the complaint procedures, a copy of the Code and a request for written reply within a 30-day time limit.

The President may also appoint the most recent past Chairman of the Committee on Professional Ethics to investigate violations of code. When warranted the Chairman will investigate and file complaints when there has been a possible violation to the Code or to the C&B codes. The Executive Director follows the procedures for these complaints in accordance with the same manner as previous complaints made. There are no special considerations given to these complaints. The Committee on Professional Ethics receives the complaint from the Executive Director after the 30-day time limit has passed. The responses are also sent to the Committee at this time. The Committee may make a decision on the complaint based on the information already obtained by the Executive Director.

Committee on Professional Ethics Proceedings

The Committee has the right to ask the Executive Director for additional information not already included in the documentation. The Committee has the right to allow the complainant and the Member in question to represent their sides of the issue in a more formal hearing. The parties may seek legal representation and there may be a period of witness cross examinations allowed. The Committee acts as the judge in these proceedings. The Committee also decides if information is relevant or not without regard to the legal rules of evidence. Once these proceedings have been finalized, the Committee is responsible for the provision of a written decision. The written decision will list the Committee's findings of fact and the conclusions that have been reached. The Member may face repercussions consisting of a slap on the wrist, or worse, a suspension of one year, or in severe cases, expulsion from the NCRA Association.

An expulsion or suspension is not given lightly. The Board of Directors considers the Constitution and the Bylaws in coming to this decision. The Board must reach a vote of two-thirds with a quorum present to execute a suspension or an expulsion. The slaps on the wrists or reprimands are held with strict confidence in accordance with Section E's complaint procedures and regulations. The Committee has ninety days after receiving the response to either issue a decision or to schedule a hearing. If a hearing is scheduled and conducted, then the Committee will have 60 days from that hearing date to issue their decision. In the case of an appeal of a decision, the parties involved will have 30 days to respond to the notification of the decision. This is not the case of a party that has received a suspension or an expulsion.

Appeal Process

The appeal process gives the parties 30 days to respond to the notification of the decision. This appeal response must be in writing and sent to the Board of Directors. The appeal must include reasons why the decision should be amended. If no appeal is requested, then the Director will send the record to the Committee and the Board of Directors. The Board makes the final determination as to whether to uphold the Committee's previous decision. If an appeal is requested, then the Director sends copies of the appeal to all parties involved in the action. Then, one of the parties may send a response within a 10-day period. At the end of the 10-day period, the Director sends all documents pertaining to the decision to the Board of Directors. The Board has the right to make the decision based on these documents.

The Board also has the right to request that a hearing be scheduled. This hearing can include verbal arguments from the counsel or the individuals involved. The Board has the right to uphold the previous decision or to overturn the previous decision. The Board's decision is the final step in this process. The costs associated with the proceedings will be incurred by those parties involved. Each party will pay their own associated costs. The Member who finds himself under a reprimand, a suspension, or an expulsion can expect to have the action publicized in accordance with the code. The Journal of Court Reporting will list the offense and the name of the person who has received the punishment. The information can only be stricken from the Journal of Court Reporting at the request of the Committee on Professional ethics. This will only be accomplished if the Member is cleared from the wrong doing.

Advisory Opinion Procedures

The Advisory Opinion Procedures has two parts. One part is the Private Advisory Opinions. The other part is the Public Advisory Opinions. The Private Advisory Opinion is an option that may be pursued instead of proceeding with a complaint. This is discussed further under the Section A (3) of the Complaint Procedures. Sometimes, this presents an alternative for persons who need to ascertain whether an action or conduct is permissible under the Code of Professional Ethics. This option allows the identity of the person seeking guidance to remain confidential. The Board of Directors may instruct otherwise in regards to the confidential status. The usual procedure maintains this air of confidentiality. The Committee may make a decision based upon the information received. However, the Committee may request further information. The Committee initiates a Public Advisory Opinions.

The Committee may provide illumination on a provision within the Code of Professional Ethics. This illumination may be based upon facts obtained from review of information in a Private Advisory Opinion. However, the pertinent details concerning the Private Advisory Opinion are not referenced in the publication. The Board of Directors maintains the rights to review, modify, or reject any Private or Public Advisory Opinion or its parts. The Public Advisory Opinions are numbered. The subjects listed can be used to help a Member determine appropriate conduct. The first Advisory Opinion has to do with the receiving of freelance work under the guise of official court reporter. The second Public Advisory Opinion has to do with reporting on depositions that are carried out by friends or family. Public Advisory Opinion number 3 gives guidelines for the hiring of substitute reporters.

Public Advisory Opinion number 3 also pertains to regulations for court reporters in cases where their spouse's law firm is connected. Public Advisory Opinion number 4 advises on the practice of altering official records. Public Advisory Opinion number 5 advises on the practice of non-payment of service to substitute reporters. Public Advisory Opinion number 6 concerns the report of a deposition when an unresolved ending is part of the record. Public Advisory Opinion number 7 advises on the practice of contracting with insurance carriers for services. Public Advisory Opinion number 8 advises on the practice of promoting the sale of transcripts at private and public proceedings. Public Advisory Opinion number 9 advises person on what to do in the case of third party sales of transcripts. Public Advisory Opinion number 9 also discusses the practice to follow regarding depositions and public records.

Public Advisory Opinion number 10 advises on the transcription services of reporters who do not work for a firm. Public Advisory Opinion number 11 advises on the practice of reporting and witnessing in a case. Public Advisory Opinion number 12 advises on the practice of reporting on a deposition where a legal opponent has a concern. Public Advisory Opinion number 13 advises on the practice of handing out gifts or incentives with monetary value. Public Advisory Opinion number 14 advises on the practice of storing and distributing disks and facts. Public Advisory Opinion number 15 advises on the practice of formulating the order of transcript deliveries. Public Advisory Opinion number 16 advises on the formulation of the order of exhibit delivery. Public Advisory Opinion number 17 advises on the practice of making contingent payment arrangements.

Public Advisory Opinion number 18 advises on the practice of making a certified ASCII disk. Public Advisory Opinion number 19 advises on the practice of changing an agency's certification page in place of a reporter's page in documents. Public Advisory Opinion number 20 advises on the practice of client delivery and receipt of an ASCII file. Public Advisory Opinion number 21 advises on the practice of changing the format around on a transcript page. Public Advisory Opinion number 22 advises on the practice of giving out portions or excerpts from testimony. Public Advisory Opinion number 23 advises on the practice of creating record of conversations or comments that are to be held off the record. Public Advisory Opinion number 24 advises on the practice of giving out names and addresses of counsel associated with a deposition to members of a third party.

Public Advisory Opinion number 25 advises on the practice of providing ASCII files and hardcopy, paper notes of documented proceedings. Public Advisory Opinion number 26 advises on the selling of transcript reproductions in open or public assemblies. Public Advisory Opinion number 27 discusses the fairness of Provision No. 8. Public Advisory Opinion number 28 advises on the practice of transcription not requested by counsel. Public Advisory Opinion number 29 discusses the obligations that agency owners have in regards towards the ethical behavior of nonmember reporters. Public Advisory Opinion number 1 uses Provisions 6 and 9 of the Code of the Professional Ethics to help freelance reporters act appropriately. Provision 6 advises avoidance of any type of freelance work that interferes with the reporter's official responsibilities. Provision 9 upholds the professionalism and honor of the position.

The Public Advisory Opinion number 1 advises the reporter to make known any relationships of a family or personal nature among the council members. This allows the counsel to request a different reporter before the proceedings start. If objections are made, then the reporter should pull out from the position. The counsel can either let the reporter find a different reporter to replace the current reporter or the counsel may pick a reporter that they prefer. Provisions that are violated under this Public Advisory Opinion number 2 are Provisions 1 and 2 of the Code of Professional Ethics. Profession 1 gives attention to how the impartiality of the reporter is displayed from the beginning to the end of each assignment. Provision 2 gives directions to the reporter to stay aware of how their associations or acquaintances can appear as a conflict of interest. The provision advises a completely open policy in making the conflict of interest known to the counsel.

The Public Advisory Opinion number 3 advises the reporter on how commissions are retained when a spousal relationship causes the reporter to give up the job. The reporter with a spousal relationship may accept a commission because there is no violation. However, if the reporter took depositions from other counsel in the spouse's firm, then that could be considered a violation. The Provisions that are violated in this case are Provisions 1 and 3 of the Code of Professional Ethics. These provisions provided impartiality and the appearance of impropriety. There are ways around these violations. One would be completely open about the relationship from the start of the beginning of the deposition. The other way would be in making sure that no one in the spouse's firm had any problems with you taking on the job. An additional consideration would be to make sure that your reporter certificate has been amended to conform to the factual information.

The Public Advisory Opinion number 4 advises the reporter on his or her responsibility in making an accurate record of the proceedings. The Provisions 1, 3, and 9 of the code of Professional Ethics addresses the violations that can occur should a reporter not fulfill this responsibility. A judge cannot instruct the reporter to add or omit portions of the record that has been made. The only way a change that can impact a ruling can be made is for the judge and the counsel to come to an agreement about the change. The motion or the agreement of all counsel can legally result in a change in the document. There can be grammatical changes made. Provision 1 state that an air of impartiality should be maintained as a reporter performs the duties of the position. Provision 3 states that the appearance of any impropriety should be avoided. Provision 9 upholds the professionalism and honor of the position.

The Public Advisory Opinion number 5 was written to address the problem of paying a fee to a substitute reporter. Substitute reporters that have performed the work do expect payment from the reporter that has contracted the work out. However, the Code of Professional Ethics was not designed to give arbitration for settlements of fees. If there is a fee dispute, the reporter is advised to file court actions against the reporter that has not lived up to the previous agreement made. The conduct of the reporter who has not paid may be made to the Board of Certified Shorthand Reporters or to state certification associations. The Professional Ethics Committee is without power or jurisdiction to involve itself between the business matters of reporters. The Professional Ethics Committee will only handle complaints that are addressed by the provisions written in the Code of Professional Ethics.

The Public Advisory Opinion number 6 advises on what to do in the case when a hiring attorney instructs the reporter to go off the record before a satisfactory conclusion has been met by all parties. The reporter should continue regardless of the hiring attorney's instruction. To stop the documentation procedures would cause the reporter to be in violation of impartiality. The proper conduct for this circumstance would be that the counsels agree upon the completion of the proceedings. Only with that ending would it be appropriate for the reporter to stop recording. The Code of Professional Ethics advises the reporter on the appropriate actions to take in case such as these. Provision 1 state that the reporter will act with impartiality and fairness in performing his or her duties. Provision 9 upholds the professionalism and honor of the position of a court reporter.

The Public Advisory Opinion number 7 advises the reporter on their associations between insurance groups. NCRA has taken the stance of neutrality on this issue. The Committee of Professional ethics wants no part of trying to determine the correctness of the relationships and contracts between the insurance groups and the reporting firms. This issue has come under the advisement of the legal counsel for NCRA. The counsel, C. Coleman Bird, suggests that the NCRA should not become involved in this problematic issue dealing with antitrust laws. The lawyer further advises that the individual should be free to determine his or her own contractual decisions. Antitrust laws do allow that members may join in lobbying efforts for governmental activation of laws to promote or prohibit the agreements that are made between reporters and insurance groups. There are no provisions that apply to this issue.

The Public Advisory Opinion number 8 advises the reporter in the sale of transcripts. The provisions which apply to this are Provision 1, 4, and 9. Provision 1 state that the reporter will act with impartiality and fairness. Provision 4 states the reporter is responsible to make sure that security and confidentiality is kept in regards to the verbal or written information given during a proceeding. Provision 9 upholds the professionalism and honor of the position. In the case of public hearings, the reporter has the right to sell a copy of the transcript to those present. However, in the case of non-public hearings, the hiring party has the right to make the determination of who can purchase the transcript and can determine how the document is distributed. The hiring party retains rights of control over the record. A reporter must seek permission for sales from the hiring party.

The Public Advisory Opinion number 9 advises the reporter in the selling of the deposition to parties other than the persons connected to the lawsuit and the persons testifying. Occasionally, a reporter wishes to sell a deposition to persons who are not part to the case. One group that may be interested in the record is the press. The reporter should ask himself about the public or non-public status of a record. The sale rights on the work in question must be determined. The Federal Rules of Civil Procedure states that the deposition is sealed until payment is received. This means that without the counsel or court order, the deposition cannot be distributed as a public record. The only persons that can have access to it those involved in the litigation and the persons testifying. The sale of the deposition without this permission is in violation of Provisions 1, 4, and 9 of the code of Ethics.

The Public Advisory Opinion number 10 advises the freelance firm on the reporting of depositions that have been initiated by a previous employed reporter. Provision numbers 5 and 9 apply in this situation. Provision 5 states that a reporter should make honest and correct factual statements. Provision 9 states that a reporter should uphold the honor and professionalism of the position. The best policy is to make certain that these agreements have already been put in place at the time an individual is hired. The Federal rules consider that it is the implied obligation of the person whom originally took the deposition to fulfill the duty of the reporter. Ethically, the firm should contact the original reporter. If the reporter refuses the position offered or cannot meet the deadline requirements, then the firm should hire an alternate reporter to complete the work. This is documented by an attached certificate page.

The Public Advisory Opinion number 11 advises on the dual positions of reporting and testifying. Provisions 1, 2, 4, and 9 are used to make the determination by the Professional Ethics Committee. Provision 1 state that the reporter will act with impartiality and fairness. Provision 2 gives directions to the reporter to stay aware of how their associations or acquaintances can appear as a conflict of interest. The provision advises a completely open policy in making the conflict of interest known to the counsel. Provision 4 states the reporter is responsible to make sure that security and confidentiality is kept in regards to the verbal or written information given during a proceeding. Provision 9 upholds the professionalism and honor of the position. The exact situations must be regarded in accordance with the provisions to determine if a violation occurs in an actual case.

The Public Advisory Opinion number 12 advises on lawsuits filed by a reporting company against an insurance group. Provisions 1, 2, 3, and 9 apply to the violation. Provision 1 state that the reporter will act with impartiality and fairness. Provision 2 gives directions to the reporter to stay aware of how their associations or acquaintances can appear as a conflict of interest. The provision advises a completely open policy in making the conflict of interest known to the counsel. Provision 3 states that any appearance of impropriety should be avoided. Provision 9 upholds the professionalism and honor of the position. If a reporter does not make full disclosure of the lawsuit and the possible conflict of interests, then the reporter will have violated Provision 2. An objection to the reporter's continued working on the case would constitute a necessary withdrawal from the case. For indirect involvements, the reporter does not need to disclose the relationship.

The Public Advisory Opinion number 13 advises on the receipt of gifts or monetary incentives in return for services rendered by a reporter. Provisions 3 and 9 address this concern. Provision 3 states that any appearance of impropriety should be avoided. Provision 9 upholds the professionalism and honor of the position. The purpose of provision 3 is to uphold the appearance of proper conduct. A gift may compromise the person's impartial standing within the community. In turn, this could reduce the person's standing as a professional within the reporting community. The Committee went on to add Provision 8 to the Code to restrict these actions. Provision 8 states that reporters should not give any gift or incentive that is more than $25.00 at a time or more than $50.00 for the year to clients or counsel members. These provisions serve to protect the reporter from any hint of misconduct.

The Public Advisory Opinion number 14 advises on the practices of disk/data retention and distribution. Provisions 3, 4, and 9 of the Professional Code of Ethics apply in these situations. Provision 3 states that any appearance of impropriety should be avoided. Provision 4 states the reporter is responsible to make sure that security and confidentiality is kept in regards to the verbal or written information given during a proceeding. Provision 9 upholds the professionalism and honor of the position. Disks and data must be handled in accordance with the same rules that apply to shorthand notes, printed transcripts, exhibits and other records. These standards can be found in the Certified Shorthand Reporter. They are also located in state, local, and federal laws. Reporters have the duty to operate as independent makers of record. That means that they must perform the duties of notary publics, and court officials.

The Public Advisory Opinion number 15 advises on the practice of submitting a deposition transcript and a diskette of the deposition transcript to a third party. The Provisions 1, 2, 3, 4, and 9 apply. Provision 1 state that the reporter will act with impartiality and fairness. Provision 2 gives directions to the reporter to stay aware of how their associations or acquaintances can appear as a conflict of interest. The provision advises a completely open policy in making the conflict of interest known to the counsel. Provision 3 states that any appearance of impropriety should be avoided. Provision 4 states the reporter is responsible to make sure that security and confidentiality is kept in regards to the verbal or written information given during a proceeding. Provision 9 upholds the professionalism and honor of the position. Reporters should not submit a deposition transcript and a diskette of the deposition transcript to a third party.

The Public Advisory Opinion number 16 advises the reporter on the practice of submitting exhibits or parts of the transcripts to members of a third party. The Provisions 1, 2, 3, 4, and 9 apply. Provision 1 state that the reporter will act with impartiality and fairness. Provision 2 gives directions to the reporter to stay aware of how their associations or acquaintances can appear as a conflict of interest. The provision advises a completely open policy in making the conflict of interest known to the counsel. Provision 3 states that any appearance of impropriety should be avoided. Provision 4 states the reporter is responsible to make sure that security and confidentiality is kept in regards to the verbal or written information given during a proceeding. Provision 9 upholds the professionalism and honor of the position. Reporters should not submit exhibits or parts of the transcripts to members of a third party.

The Public Advisory Opinion number 17 advises the reporter on the practice of contingency fees on reporting services. Provisions 1, 3, and 9 apply. Provision 1 state that the reporter will act with impartiality and fairness. Provision 3 states that any appearance of impropriety should be avoided. Provision 9 upholds the professionalism and honor of the position. A contingency fee means that the reporter is only paid if the client of the hiring party reaches a favorable outcome in the proceedings. This practice can be harmful to the reporter's ability to remain neutral within a proceeding. This can be seen as a violation of Provision 1 and 3. The reporter's financial wellbeing relies on the favorable outcome for the hiring party and jeopardizes the reporter's role as "official of the court". The reporter should not enter into an arrangement that provides contingency fees with the hiring party.

The Public Advisory Opinion number 18 advises the reporter on certification of ASCII disks that contain a transcript of the hearing and has references the subject of contents certifications. This refers to the certification of an ASCII disk with the recorded transcription. The reporter should also keep the original notes of the proceeding to further give validation of the information obtained. The reporter can expect that the contents may be used to verify the information recorded on the ASCII disk. This step further ensures the accuracy on the ASCII disk. The certification procedures further record the date of that the original transcription was made. The ASCII disk version should be recorded within the original transcription to further ensure security and validation of the information. A label may be attached to the disk along with a cover letter with the certification information included within its contents.

The Public Advisory Opinion number 19 advises the reporter on out of state reporting arrangements. Provisions 3, 5 and 9 address this concern. Provision 3 states that any appearance of impropriety should be avoided. Provision 5 states that a reporter should make honest and correct factual statements. Provision 9 upholds the professionalism and honor of the position. The Committee of Professional Ethics do not condone this practice. This practice may be a violation of federal, state, and local law regarding the certification of transcripts. The reporter should carefully ascertain whether the proper certification procedures are maintained. The reporter's certification page should be attached to the hardcopies and the ASCII disks. Sometimes, the out of state agencies may replace its certification page cover for the certification page of the transcriber legally. If legal procedures are not followed, the reporter would be wise in not accepting the assignment from the out of state reporting agency.

The Public Advisory Opinion number 20 advises on time delivery of the ASCII disk and transcripts. Provisions 3 and 9 apply to the violation of failing to deliver on time. Provision 3 states that any appearance of impropriety should be avoided. Provision 9 upholds the professionalism and honor of the position. The Committee of Professional Ethics do not condone this practice. The reporter has a responsibility to ensure that the document is delivered on time. The agency may be late in getting the document to the client. In this case, the reporter must let the agency know that the reporter is going to deliver the document to the client. The reporter should make sure that the document is delivered to the client as arranged. This will ensure that the reporter has completed his or her work as a subcontractor for the agency and avoids the violations.

The Public Advisory Opinion number 21 advises on not creating a document with more pages for the express purpose of overcharging a consumer for a less than adequate product. This could be construed as deceptive advertising. Provisions 5 and 9 apply to the violation of deceptive advertising. Provision 5 states that a reporter should make honest and correct factual statements. Provision 9 upholds the professionalism and honor of the position. The Committee of Professional Ethics do not condone this practice. The reporter should not practice deception in allowing the consumer to believe that the document requires more pages simply because a different format has been used. If the reporter is unsure of what format to use, then the reporter should follow the Transcript Format Guidelines that were printed in 1992. These guidelines were published to allow the reporter the opportunity to follow these recommendations. These guidelines are suggestions and not required to be followed.

The Public Advisory Opinion number 22 advises on the use of partial testimonies in a deposition. A provision 1 applies to the violation on the use of such excerpts. Provision 1 state that the reporter will act with impartiality and fairness. The Committee further advises that the reporter make every effort to use a two-part disclosure process if an action is requested. This disclosure should begin before the next day's proceedings. The reporter must inform the hiring attorney of the request for an excerpt to the testimony. All parties must be given notice so that they may purchase the excerpts. If the excerpt is still requested, then the reporter gives the other party the opportunity to request transcript excerpts that they may require, as well as the one originally requested by the hiring counsel. The reporter is responsible for delivery of these requested documents.

The Public Advisory Opinion number 23 advises on the reporter's responsibility in regards to "off the record" conversations. Provisions 1, 3, and 9 apply to the violation of such responsibilities. Provision 1 state that the reporter will act with impartiality and fairness. Provision 3 states that any appearance of impropriety should be avoided. Provision 9 upholds the professionalism and honor of the position. The Committee of Professional Ethics do not condone this practice. The reporter should not make a record of these conversations once a deposition has ended. The counsel requesting information about the conversations must subpoena the reporter for testimony. The reporter is subject to the same rules that apply to witnesses of courts. To create a record of the "off the record" conversations would be unethical. The reporter should refuse to participate in creating such a document as requested by the deposing counsel.

The Public Advisory Opinion number 24 advises on the reporting firm's responsibility in furnishing names and addresses of lawyers to other lawyers involved in a legal action. Provisions 4 and 9 apply to the violation involved in providing this contact information. Provision 4 states the reporter is responsible to make sure that security and confidentiality is kept in regards to the verbal or written information given during a proceeding. Provision 9 upholds the professionalism and honor of the position. The prior consent of the parties being disclosed must be given to prevent this violation. The reporting firm has a responsibility of maintaining a confidential status for the parties involved unless the disclosure has been given prior permission. The Federal Rules of Civil Procedure apply in this case. The reporter can make deposition transcripts available only to those parties that were involved with the legal proceeding in question.

The Public Advisory Opinion number 25 advises on arrangements made in regards to out-of-state reporting. Provision 4 applies to violations possible in this case. Provision 4 states the reporter is responsible to make sure that the security and confidentiality is kept in regards to the verbal or written information given during a proceeding. The freelance reporter may be engaged to provide hardcopy notes on a disposition transcript, as well as the ASCII disk. The reporter should make sure to keep a hardcopy file on the notes sent. This action further ensures the security of the information that has been provided. This security measure prevents the transcript from being changed or deleted in the future. This act of keeping a secure hardcopy file of the notes on the transcript is also subject to many state and local legislature. The reporter should not violate the trust that has been placed in him or her.

The Public Advisory Opinion number 26 advises on the sale of copies of a transcript to the audience. Provisions 4 apply to the violation involved in providing this sale. Provision 4 states the reporter is responsible to make sure that security and confidentiality is kept in regards to the verbal or written information given during a proceeding. If a hiring counsel gives permission for the sale of copies of a transcript to the audience involved in the legal meeting, then the reporter has the authority to make the sale. However, when that is not given, the reporter risks violation of Provision 4 in making that sale. The reporter may also want to reflect upon the Public Advisory Opinion number 8's suggestion of avoiding problems beforehand. A good suggestion would be to seek the permission of the hiring counsel prior to the proceeding or the sale.

The Public Advisory Opinion number 27 advises on the practice of accepting gifts. This Advisory amends and supersedes the Advisory Opinion number 13. In addition, the Provision 8 may apply in this case. Provision 8 states that members shall not accept or be the givers for gifts of more than \$25.00 per transaction. The limit on these transactions shall amount to \$50.00 in any aggregate year. Subsequently, this amount was increased from \$50.00 to a \$100.00 amount. The limit of \$25.00 was eliminated completed. The annual limit left was the only cautionary guideline. This practice of giving and receiving gifts may lead to a circumstance that places the reporter in a compromised role. Therefore, the board advises that the reporter remain impartial and avoid the look of compromised behavior. However, the nominal item limitations have been set to prevent any suggestion of any impropriety. There is no disfavor if these guidelines are followed.

The Public Advisory Opinion number 28 advises on the procedures guiding the request of a transcript of an official record of legal proceedings. The Provisions 1, 3, and 9 may apply to this case. Provision 1 state that the reporter will act with impartiality and fairness. Provision 3 states that any appearance of impropriety should be avoided. Provision 9 upholds the professionalism and honor of the position. The Committee of Professional Ethics do not condone this practice. The reporter should provide all parties with disclosure recording the request and availability of the requested documented. These records must be made available to all parties once the request has been made. The reporter has an obligation to maintain a high standard of ethical integrity in his or her relationship with the client. This ethical integrity allows the reporter to remain professional, impartial, and respected within the legal community.

The Public Advisory Opinion number 29 advises on the freelance firms and reporters that work for the firm that are not NCRA members. Provision 9 applies in these cases. Provision 9 upholds the professionalism and honor of the position. The Committee of Professional Ethics do not condone this practice. NCRA membership gives the freelance firm the opportunity to know that their reporters have qualified for the position of reporter. To hire a person that has not qualified for the NCRA membership would constitute a lack of integrity by the firm. Circumvention of the Professional Code of Ethics by this means can imply that the owner is in violation of Provision 9. It does not mean that the firm is always responsible for the conduct of the independent contractors in which it hires. Firms should assign experienced reporters for the tasks that they are qualified to handle.

NCRA Contracting Disclosure Policy

The NCRA Contracting Disclosure Policy has been broken down into four statements. The first paragraph explains the procedure for disclosing information about relationships that the reporter may have before a case begins. The reporter should report indirect and direct relationships so that the counsel will have the opportunity to exercise their rights. The rights are listed under the Rules 28©, 29 and 32(d) (2) under the Federal Rules of Civil Procedure. The deposition could be disqualified if these rules are not adhered. The disclosure includes the identifications of all persons involved in the contracting firm and associations. The disclosure will list a complete set of descriptions of all work assignments performed by the reporter and its firm. The second paragraph denotes the equality of work that is provided to all parties involved. This will allow an exchange of comparable services only. Healthy competition among court reporters is encouraged.

The NCRA Contracting Disclosure Policies remaining two statements are found in paragraphs 3 and 4. Paragraph 3 explains how a court reporter should refrain from performing a role of advocacy for either party involved in litigation. The reporter has his or her appearance of impartiality and neutrality to maintain. In paragraph 4 the reporter is advised to follow the federal, state, and local laws. These laws pertain to the behaviors and conducts that are necessary for a court reporter to maintain. The rules will give the court reporter a clear understanding of how to handle certification issues. The rules will give the court reporter a basis for dealing with confidentiality issues. The rules will describe how to handle the custody of transcripts in a professional manner. Plus, the rules will discuss the issues and proper methods involved with subcontracting work.

The response of the US Department of Justice to the NCRA Contracting Disclosure Policy was favorable. Previously, in Paragraph number 1 the procedure for disclosing information about relationships that the reporter may have before a case begins. The reporter should report indirect and direct relationships so that the counsel will have the opportunity to exercise their rights. The rights are listed under the Rules 28©, 29 and 32(d) (2) under the Federal Rules of Civil Procedure. The deposition could be disqualified if these rules are not adhered. The disclosure includes the identifications of all persons involved in the contracting firm and associations. The disclosure will list a complete set of descriptions of all work assignments performed by the reporter and its firm. This paragraph was strengthened to provide justifiable "disqualification for interest" of the court reporter. Objections can be made on the grounds that the relationship interferes with the reporters' ability to be impartial.

The response of the US Department of Justice to the NCRA Contracting Disclosure Policy was favorable. Previously, in the second paragraph the equality of work that is provided to all parties involved was determined. Reporters must continue to make every effort to provide this exchange of comparable services to the parties involved. Healthy competition among court reporters was still encouraged. This is not intended to become a way to limit competition through the disclosure of services and prices charged. The US Department of Justice agreed that the reporter should not provide special arrangements to one party without providing those same services to the other party involved. The court reporter cannot just disclose the information without following suit with an appropriate action. This allowed an exchange of comparable services for both parties involved in the litigation and avoided violation of antitrust laws.

The response of the US Department of Justice to the NCRA Contracting Disclosure Policy was favorable. Previously, in the third paragraph the explanation was provided on how a court reporter should refrain from performing a role of advocacy for either party involved in litigation. The reporter has his or her appearance of impartiality and neutrality to maintain. This was again reiterated in that the court reporter had to walk a fine line in providing state of the art technology to individuals while maintaining a comparable service to all parties involved. The reporter should avoid all hints of partiality and keep from showing favoritism with one party over another. To do so, would hint of the reporter as being on the side of one party in the litigation. The air of impartiality and neutrality would be lost.

The response of the US Department of Justice to the NCRA Contracting Disclosure Policy was favorable. Previously, in the fourth paragraph 4 the reporter is advised to follow the federal, state, and local laws. These laws pertain to the behaviors and conducts that are necessary for a court reporter to maintain. The rules will give the court reporter a clear understanding of how to handle certification issues. The rules will give the court reporter a basis for dealing with confidentiality issues. The rules will describe how to handle the custody of transcripts in a professional manner. Plus, the rules will discuss the issues and proper methods involved with subcontracting work. The response of the US Department of Justice upheld these policies. The federal, state, and local laws offer a sound basis for the operations of a court reporter.

English Vocabulary

Abate: lessen or to fade away.

Abjure: renounce or to swear off under oath.

Abortive: to stop because of a lack of success.

Abstinence: teetotalism or self-discipline.

Abstruse: obscure or difficult to understand.

Accede: to consent or agree upon.

Adamant: unyielding about a matter.

Adjunct: addition or an appendage.

Adversity: a situation of misfortune or bad luck.

Affinity: kinship or bond.

Anomaly: an irregularity or variation.

Arbitrary: to decide without regard to the law in an autocratic or arrogant manner.

Ardent: to have a passion or zeal about something.

Askance: sideways or with suspicion.

Assay: test or examine

Assuage: to accede to somebody's demands in hopes of appeasement.

Augur: a soothsayer or fortune-teller with clairvoyant abilities.

Avow: to declare or to acknowledge.

Blandishment: flattery or coaxing.

Blithe: cheerful or happy go lucky attitude.

Boorish: ill-mannered or churlish.

Brier: patch or mend a hole.

Calumny: slander or misrepresent.

Caprice: a whim or desire to change without apparent cause.

Caustic: acrimonious or sarcastic.

Chide: to scold or reprimand.

Clandestine: a secret or secluded meeting.

Compress: to condense something in order to make it smaller.

Condemn: scorn

Cumbersome: an unwieldy or burdensome object.

Curb: to restrain or stop yourself from doing something.

Cursory: hasty or perfunctory manner.

Decadent: decaying or declining.

Decree: an edict or an announcement.

Deflect: divert or turn aside.

Deleterious: harmful or lethal condition.

Delude: to mislead or give the wrong impression about something or someone.

Demure: a modest or unpretentious state of being.

Despoil: an act of plundering or vandalism.

Digress: to branch or divert from the original intention.

Disconsolate: downhearted or discouraged in demeanor.

Dissemble: tear down or beat around the bush.

Disseminate: to scatter or spread out widely.

Draconian: severe.

Ebb: the spot where a decline or a drop is indicated.

Ebullient: effervescent or jovial.

Elucidate: clarify or state in obvious terminology.

Elysian: blissful or delightful.

Emancipate: set free or release.

Encroach: to trespass or to infringe upon someone else's rights.

Endow: to give or bestow something onto someone else.

Enigma: a puzzle or mysterious statement.

Epistle: letter or missive.

Equanimity: composure or evenness of mind.

Equitable: fair or equal in some fashion.

Expiate: atone or make amends.

Explicit: clear or unambiguous statement.

Extricate: to disentangle oneself.

Farce: swindle or a ridiculous situation.

Fatuous: pointless and inane sensibility.

Feeble: weak or delicate.

Fervent: earnest or enthusiastic.

Flaccid: flabby or overweight.

Flagrant: a glaring or scandalous quality.

Frugal: a thrifty or inexpensive way of spending money in an attempt to save person money.

Fungible: interchangeable.

Gamut: range or extent.

Garish: showy or gaudy in appearance.

Gauche: an awkward or tactless mannerism.

Gaunt: to have an appearance of leanness or starvation about one.

Glib: slick or polished manner.

Glutton: person with a voracious appetite.

Gregarious: sociable or enjoy being with others.

Haphazard: coincidental or unsystematic.

Haughty: to have an attitude of superiority or arrogance towards others.

Hoodwink: a trick or pull the wool over somebody's eyes.

Hue: color or tone.

Hummock: knoll

Hypocritical: insincere or phony.

Immaculate: spotlessly clean or neat as a pin.

Imminent: an impending or sudden occurrence.

Impasse: a deadlock or a stalemate.

Impediment: an obstacle or barrier that presents a difficulty of some type.

Implacable: unappeasable or unquenchable desire.

Infuse: pervade or saturate.

Ingenuous: naïve or sincere.

Inimical: hostile or unfriendly.

Inordinate: excessive or unwarranted.

Insidious: treacherous or sinister.

Invective: a defamation or foul language.

Invigorate: a description of stimulation or enlivenment.

Jovial: jolly.

Keelhaul: scold or haul a person under the keel of a ship to harm or punish.

Kowtow: to bow or do the accepted thing.

Labored: strained or strenuous.

Lacerate: to tear or to slash.

Lament: regret

Lassitude: languor or having a lack of energy.

Lien: garnish or legal claim on a property in lieu of payments on a debt.

Lionize: glorify or treat as a celebrity.

Lope: to gallop or to sprint.

Lucid: clear or well-structured thought.

Machination: machinery or having a mechanical property.

Maelstrom: whirlpool off the coast of Norway or a description of a swirling mass of feelings.

Martial: warlike or soldierly manner.

Middling: to be moderate or passable

Militant: aggressive or belligerent.

Mitigate: lessen or mollify in some manner.

Moderate: reasonable or fair.

Molten: a condition that occurs through a process of melting and casting a material.

Necropolis: cemetery or graveyard.

Nefarious: wicked or disreputable.

Nemesis: retribution or vengeance.

Noxious: harmful or deleterious.

Oblique: a slanting or angled shape.

Obsequious: servile or obedient out of hopeful expectation or fear of something or someone.

Obtuse: unperceptive or blunt manner.

Onus: burden or responsibility.

Opprobrious: shameful or expression of scorn.

Overweening: cocky or haughty manner.

Palanquin: a litter or a seat hung on poles carried upon the shoulders of men.

Paragon: model with an excellent measure of distinction.

Pastoral: rustic or bucolic.

Pecuniary: having to do with economics or financial matters.

Perfidious: treacherous or deceitful in nature.

Peripatetic: itinerant

Pernicious: lethal or insidious.

Ploy: a stratagem or gambit.

Poise: composure or self-confidence.

Polemic: argumentative.

Precipitous: steep or precipice.

Precocious: bright or gifted.

Prescience: forethought or foreknowledge

Primp: adorn.

Prodigal: extravagant or lavish practices.

Profligate: libertine.

Profuse: a bountiful abundance.

Propensity: a tendency to do something.

Propound: propose or bring forward.

Prorogue: postpone.

Punctilious: exact or precise attention to details.

Purloin: steal

Recondite: difficult or out of the way.

Rectitude: integrity or morality.

Resent: be offended.

Reticent: taciturn or uncommunicative

Retort: answer or come back with a snappy reply.

Rogue: a scoundrel or rascal type character.

Rubicund: ruddy or reddish in color.

Ruminate: ponder or think deeply.

Ruse: trick or scam.

Sacrament: ritual or atonement.

Scourge: whip or thorn in your side.

Sedulous: persevering or unrelenting about a matter.

Seedling: young or immature vegetation.

Sentience: a consciousness or capacity for feeling emotions.

Shrewd: clever or on the ball.

Slake: satisfy or quench.

Smite: strike or slash.

Solvent: creditworthy

Spare: thin or insubstantial.

Spurious: false or untrue.

Stentorian: very loud or prevailing sound.

Stolid: impassive or unable to be moved.

Strident: vociferous or harsh.

Stunt: hinder or hold back.

Superfluous: excessive or surplus to requirements.

Surfeit: an excessive or disproportionate amount of something.

Sustenance: nourishment that strengthens the body.

Sycophant: toady or flatterer.

Tacit: silent or unstated.

Taciturn: being silent or having little to say.

Tedious: dull.

Temerity: rashness or impertinence.

Thespian: actor or theatrical.

Thrash: beat or flog.

Thriftless: wasteful with no thought of frugality

Tortuous: crooked or twisting.

Truculent: fierce or confrontational.

Ubiquitous: omnipresent or being everywhere at once.

Ulterior: hidden or concealed.

Undulate: swing or roll.

Unseemly: inappropriate or unbecoming.

Utopia: paradise or place where the laws are perfect.

Vapid: insipid or tasteless.

Veracity: honesty or authenticity.

Vigilance: a watchful state of alertness.

Vim: vitality

Virulent: poisonous or powerful.

Vituperate: berate.

Volatile: unstable or explosive.

Voluble: the tendency to be very talkative.

Voracious: insatiable or greedy.

Vow: pledge or give your promise.

Vulpine: cunning or like a fox.

Warp: bend or go out of shape.

Wary: cautious or on your guard.

Whet: to sharpen or stimulate.

Practice Spelling These Words

Spell: accessible

Spell: accessory

Spell: accidentally

Spell: accommodate

Spell: accrued

Spell: accumulate

Spell: achieve

Spell: achievement

Spell: affidavit

Spell: allotment

Spell: allotted

Spell: alumni

Spell: analyses

Spell: analysis

Spell: Antarctic

Spell: appraisal

Spell: argument

Spell: assassin

Spell: assistance

Spell: athletes

Spell: attacked

Spell: auxiliary

Spell: bachelor

Spell: bacteria

Spell: bankruptcy

Spell: barbarous

Spell: battalion

Spell: beneficially

Spell: beneficiary

Spell: benefited

Spell: bombastic

Spell: bookkeeper

Spell: boundary

Spell: briefs

Spell: brother-in-laws

Spell: calamity

Spell: calculate

Spell: calendar

Spell: calumny

Spell: camouflage

Spell: carburetor

Spell: casualty

Spell: categorical

Spell: category

Spell: caterpillar

Spell: chauffeur

Spell: chrysanthemum

Spell: clientele

Spell: collateral

Spell: combustion

Spell: commitment

Spell: comptroller

Spell: concede

Spell: conducive

Spell: confiscate

Spell: conglomerate

Spell: connoisseur

Spell: consanguinity

Spell: conscience

Spell: conscientious

Spell: conscious

Spell: consensus

Spell: continence

Spell: coolly

Spell: coordinate

Spell: coronation

Spell: corroborate

Spell: corrugate

Spell: courteous

Spell: crises

Spell: cryogenic

Spell: culpable

Spell: decadent

Spell: deferred

Spell: deficit

Spell: definite

Spell: delicatessen

Spell: deliverable

Spell: denigrate

Spell: dependent

Spell: derivative

Spell: desirable

Spell: despair

Spell: deteriorate

Spell: development

Spell: dexterous

Spell: diagnoses

Spell: Diasporas

Spell: differing

Spell: dilapidated

Spell: dilemma

Spell: dilettante

Spell: diphtheria

Spell: disappear

Spell: disappoint

Spell: disastrous

Spell: discourse

Spell: discretion

Spell: disheveled

Spell: disingenuous

Spell: dispel

Spell: dissatisfied

Spell: dissect

Spell: dissension

Spell: dissident

Spell: drowned

Spell: drunkenness

Spell: ecstasy

Spell: ecumenical

Spell: editor-in-chiefs

Spell: eligible

Spell: embarrass

Spell: eminent

Spell: endeavor

Spell: environment

Spell: equipped

Spell: etiquette

Spell: existence

Spell: existential

Spell: exorbitant

Spell: extinction

Spell: February

Spell: Filipino

Spell: flowery

Spell: forcible

Spell: forfeit

Spell: forty

Spell: fraudulent

Spell: freight

Spell: frolicsome

Spell: galvanize

Spell: gardener

Spell: gauge

Spell: genealogy

Spell: government

Spell: governor

Spell: grammar

Spell: grateful

Spell: grievance

Spell: grievous

Spell: halves

Spell: handkerchief

Spell: harass

Spell: harasses

Spell: harelip

Spell: hearsay

Spell: height

Spell: hesitant

Spell: hypocrisy

Spell: idiosyncrasy

Spell: illegible

Spell: immaculate

Spell: inadvertent

Spell: inaugurate

Spell: incessant

Spell: incidentally

Spell: incongruent

Spell: indescribable

Spell: indispensable

Spell: inertia

Spell: innocuous

Spell: insistent

Spell: installment

Spell: intercede

Spell: intermittent

Spell: irrelevant

Spell: irreligious

Spell: irresistible

Spell: jeopardize

Spell: jewelry

Spell: judgment

Spell: judiciary

Spell: knives

Spell: laboratory

Spell: labyrinth

Spell: laundry

Spell: leaves

Spell: legislate

Spell: liaison

Spell: library

Spell: lieutenant

Spell: likeable

Spell: liquidate

Spell: literature

Spell: livelihood

Spell: logistics

Spell: mannequin

Spell: marginal

Spell: mathematics

Spell: maximum

Spell: mimicry

Spell: mischievous

Spell: misspelled

Spell: mortgage

Spell: murmured

Spell: nickel

Spell: ninety

Spell: noncommittal

Spell: nonsense

Spell: obscene

Spell: occasion

Spell: occurrence

Spell: occurring

Spell: omission

Spell: omitted

Spell: overachieve

Spell: panicked

Spell: panicky

Spell: parallel

Spell: peculiarly

Spell: perfunctory

Spell: perjury

Spell: permanent

Spell: permissible

Spell: perseverance

Spell: personify

Spell: personnel

Spell: perspiration

Spell: pertinent

Spell: petition

Spell: photosynthesis

Spell: physician

Spell: picnicked

Spell: plausible

Spell: playwright

Spell: plentitude

Spell: pneumatic

Spell: pockmark

Spell: precipitate

Spell: prejudice

Spell: prerogative

Spell: preventative

Spell: privilege

Spell: procedure

Spell: proceed

Spell: procumbent

Spell: professor

Spell: prominent

Spell: pronunciation

Spell: propitiations

Spell: prosecute

Spell: psychology

Spell: publicly

Spell: pursue

Spell: pursuit

Spell: questionnaire

Spell: queue

Spell: rambunctious

Spell: rapport

Spell: recompense

Spell: recurrence

Spell: redemption

Spell: reforestation

Spell: regrettable

Spell: regurgitate

Spell: renovate

Spell: repercussions

Spell: repetition

Spell: requisition

Spell: reserved

Spell: resolute

Spell: resonance

Spell: responsive

Spell: rhythm

Spell: ridicule

Spell: ridiculous

Spell: roommate

Spell: sacrosanct

Spell: salable

Spell: salivate

Spell: secretary

Spell: seized

Spell: separate

Spell: sergeant

Spell: serviceable

Spell: siege

Spell: simultaneous

Spell: solicitous

Spell: solidify

Spell: sophomore

Spell: stimuli

Spell: stodgy

Spell: subsistence

Spell: suffrage

Spell: superfluous

Spell: superintendent

Spell: supersede

Spell: supple

Spell: suppress

Spell: surprise

Spell: surreal

Spell: surreptitious

Spell: synonymous

Spell: tariff

Spell: temerity

Spell: temperature

Spell: tentative

Spell: tertiary

Spell: theological

Spell: tragedy

Spell: umbrella

Spell: unanimous

Spell: unfortunately

Spell: usable

Spell: vacuum

Spell: vicious

Spell: villain

Spell: visible

Spell: whereas

Spell: wield

Spell: withhold

Spell: wives

Spell: yield

Important Grammar Rules

One rule states that a main verb may have an additional verb which is called an auxiliary verb. Verbs describe an action or a state of being. Another rule of grammar states that a preposition must have an object. A preposition is a word that shows relationships between other words. The object of a preposition is the word or the group of words which the action of the verb is aimed towards. For example, "She threw the ball at her mother's car." "Ball is the object of the word, "threw". In some cases, a verb may have its own object. You can locate the direct object in a sentence when you find the word that follows an action verb. The definition of a gerund is a verbal adjective used as a noun. An infinitive may be used as a noun or as adjectives.

Infinitives are a form of a verb that is not limited by a person or a number. Prepositional phrases are most often used as adjectives. Adjectives are words used to restrict or limit a noun or a pronoun. Appositives are nouns placed with other nouns as explanations. Appositives are used to replace or substitute the case of the noun that it renames. Clauses have a subject and a verb.

Compound sentences have two or more main clauses. A main clause is independent. Another grammatical rule states that a subordinate clause may use a noun, adjective, or adverb. The present participle of a verb can be located by finding the verb that ends in the letters "ing". Another grammatical rule states that an adverb is unable to modify another pronoun. Pronouns are words used in place of a noun. Another grammatical rule states that a predicate nominative will rename the subject.

Medical Vocabulary

alb: white

algia: pain

ante: before; in front of

arteri(o): artery

arthr(o): joint

articul: joint

auto: self

bio: life

brady: slow

cardi: heart

centesis: puncture

cervico: neck

chir: hand

chol: bile

cide: kill

circum: around

contra: against

cost: rib

cyan: blue

cyst(o): bladder

cyte: cell

dactyl: finger, toe

deca: ten

derm: skin

dipl: double

emia: blood

enceph: brain

erythr: red

etio: cause

eu: normal

galact: milk

gastro: stomach

geus: taste

gingivleu: gum

gloss: tongue

glyc(o): sweetness; glucose

gyn: woman

hepat: liver

hydro: water

hyper: above normal

itis: inflammation

kine: energy

leuko: white; colorless

lip(o): fat

lith: stone, calculus

lysis: break down or detatch

mal: bad

mast: breast

mega: large

melano: dark

mesi: middle

metry: process of measuring

myo: muscle

neo: new

neur: nerve

ocul: eye

odont: tooth

ology: study of

oma: tumor

omo: shoulder

oo: egg; relating to ovary

ortho: straight; upright

os: bone; a mouth/opening

oto: ear

pathy: disease of

ped: foot; child

per: through

peri: around

phil: having an affinity/love for

phleb: vein

pil: hair

pnea: breath

polio: gray

pseud: false

ptosis: displaced downward

pyr(o): heat, fire

quadr: four

ren: kidney

retro: backward

rhino: nose

rrhea: flow

sangui: blood

sclera: hard

sphygm: pulse

spondyl: vertebra

tachy: rapid

thanato: death

thromb: clot

trans: across

ven: vein

Musculoskeletal System

ankylosis: this term refers to a stiffening condition within the joint.

arm: the ulna, the radius, and the humerus are the bones which consist of this part of the body.

atlas: this refers to the term that describes the first vertebra that is responsible for supporting the skull.

atrophied: the condition that refers to a reduction in size.

axis: this term refers to the second cervical vertebra found within the spine.

brachial: portion of the body that is also known as the upper arm.

bursae: this term refers to the sacs of fluid beside the joints that reduce friction during movement.

callus: the bony deposit that surrounds a fracture in order to help the restoration process.

carpus: this term refers to the wrist.

chiroplasty: operation that describes the plastic surgery which can be performed on the hand.

clavicle: this term refers to the collarbone.

coccyx: this term refers to the tailbone found within the body.

comminuted: something (specifically a fractured bone) that has been broken into several pieces

compound: a fracture or break within the bone that has an external wound connected to the fracture.

costectomy: this describes when a rib has been removed from the body.

coxalgia: this refers to a condition of pain within the hip area of the body.

cranium: the temporal, the frontal, and the parietal make up the bones within this portion of the body.

crepitus: the sound (crackling) that is made when the fractured endings of the bones rub against each other.

cuneiforms: three wedge shaped bones located in the middle of the foot.

diaphysis: the long shaft portion of a bone.

disc: this refers to the part of the structure system between the bones vertebrae which cushion the bone.

distal: away from the center of the body; the part of a limb farthest from point of attachment

dorsal spine: also known as the thoracic spine. These 12 vertebrae make up the longest portion of the three sections of the spine.

epiphysis: the portion of the long bone that is on the end.

False ribs: the five lower ribs that are attached by cartilage to the sternum but don't directly attach.

femur: this term refers to the upper leg bone within the skeletal system that has the characteristics of being the biggest and hardiest within the body.

frontal: the anterior (front) of the body; forehead

gastrocnemius: the posterior lower leg (calf) muscle.

glenoid fossa: The bone depression on the scapula that fits the head of the humerus.

greenstick fracture: this is a break in a bone in which one side is fractured and the other side is bent. Commonly seen in children.

hamstrings: this is the portion of the body (tendons or muscle) that is back of the upper leg.

ilium: this term refers to the hipbone.

impacted: this describes the condition in where a fracture is firmly impelled into another fracture.

Inferior maxilla: the bone that is referred to as the mandible.

Instep: the upper side of the foot which is also referred to as the dorsal.

leg: the fibula, the tibia, and the femur make up the bones within this portion of the body.

Ligaments: the bands of fibrous materials that connect the bones within the body.

Lordosis: a swayback shape to the spine.

malar: this term refers to the cheekbone found in the facial area.

malleoli: this is located within the ankle.

mandible: this term refers to the jawbone.

metacarpals: there are ten of these bones in the skeletal hands.

metatarsus: five bones that rest between the instep and the toes within the foot's skeletal system.

nucleus pulposus: the inner portion of the body an intervertebral disc.

occipital fracture: this is a condition in which the back of the head has received a fracture.

omitis: describes a painful, inflammation to the shoulder area.

ossify: when substance develops to form a bone.

osteomyelitis: the condition which is indicative of inflammation of the marrow found within the bone.

osteoporosis: a softening of the bones within the skeletal system of the body.

patella: this term refers to the kneecap.

pectorals: these are the muscles located within the chest area.

periosteum: the membrane or casing which surrounds the bone.

phalanges: bones in the toes and the fingers.

plantar flexion: this term describes the curling of the toes in a downward growth.

popliteal: the portion of the body that is describing the knee.

pubic girdle: the ischium, the ilium, and the pubis make up this portion of the body.

ramus: like a branch.

reduction: this refers to the action of positioning and setting a fractured bone to begin the mending process.

rotator cuff: structure around the ball and socket shoulder joint including tendons and four muscles.

sacrum: portion of the lower end of the spine that joins with the ilium

sagittal: this refers to the sutures or fibrous bands that are located between the parietal bones in the skull; the longitudinal plane of the body that divides into left and right sections

scapula: this term refers to the shoulder blade within the body.

Scoliosis: a shape or curvature to the spine that grows abnormally from side to side.

sequestrum: this term refers to a portion of dead bone.

sphenoid: this is a hollow bony structure in the skull that encompasses part of the air sinuses.

sphincter: a muscle that has the appearance of a ring and a purpose of constriction of a passage of orifice.

spinal cord: the thick cord of nerves that is located from the medulla through the lumbar vertebra.

spontaneous fracture: condition which describes a break in the bone because of a disease.

Sternum: the bone referred to as the breastbone that protects the tissues underneath.

subluxation: the description of a partial dislocation of the bones.

supinators: the muscles within the forearms that allow for the movement of turning the palms in an upward position.

supraclavicular: this term refers to the area above the clavicle.

suture: this term refers to the fibrous joint within the body.

tarsus: the portion of bone located within the foot.

thoracic: of the chest; this refers to the part of the spine also known as the dorsal vertebrae.

tibia: this term refers to the shinbone.

Heart and Circulatory

anemia: the term used to describe the condition of a low degree of red corpuscles of hemoglobin in the bloodstream.

aneurysm: used to describe a widening in the artery.

angina pectoris: the brief periods of substernal pain within the heart area

aorta: big artery exiting the left ventricle of the heart.

apex: the tip portion of a cone structure, such as the heart bottom of the heart or top of lungs.

arteries: the vessels used to transport oxygenated blood throughout the body.

arterioles: the small subdivisions consisting of millions of tiny branches that allow corpuscles to pass through one at a time.

arteriosclerosis: the condition in which the arterial wall is thick and has an inelastic quality.

atrium: the term given for the superior, smaller chambers located in the heart.

blue blood: the term used to describe the blood that is without oxygen and contained within the veins.

bradycardia: slow heartbeat.

diaphragm: the muscle separating the thoracic and abdominal cavities which aids in breathing.

embolism: a term that refers to a loose blood clot that has the ability to move to other parts within the body.

endocardium: the innermost lining around the heart.

erythrocyte: used to refer to a red blood cell.

hematoma: a localized mass consisting of an effusion of blood.

hemoglobin: the protein substance in the red blood cells that carries oxygen.

hemophiliac: a person that has a hereditary disease in which the blood does not clot normally.

hemorrhage: a term that refers to an unusual discharge of blood from the circulatory system.

infarct: the area within the tissue that has died off due to a lack of blood supply.

ischemia: the condition that exists when sufficient blood is not being supplied to an organ.

Jugular veins: the large veins of the neck (four total) that return blood from the neck and the head to the vena cava.

laryngoscope: a mirrored tool used to look at the larynx.

left ventricle: this ventricle is used to pump the blood out throughout the body and through the aorta.

leukemia: a deadly disease that consists of an overabundance of white corpuscles in the blood stream.

leukocyte: a tiny white blood cell that attacks germs that cause disease.

lymphocyte: a colorless cell located in the lymphatic organs.

mitral stenosis: the narrowed valve within the heart and circulatory system.

Mitral valve: this valve carries the oxygenated blood into the left ventricle of the heart.

murmur: the unusual sound heart on auscultation of the heart.

myocarditis: a term that refers to the condition an irritation and inflammation of the heart muscle.

Normal sinus rhythm: the term used to refer to a normal heartbeat pattern in the heart.

occlusion: a term that refers to a blockage within the circulatory system.

pacemaker: another name for this is the sinoatrial node.

palpitation: the description of the heart rhythm that feels as if the heart is fluttering like a butterfly.

pericardium: the fragile membranous sac or casing filled with serous fluid, which surrounds the heart.

plasma: a fluid portion of blood which contains fibrin and other elements.

popliteal artery: a tube that carries blood located near the knee.

Pulmonary artery: the artery which receives the blood that is pumped out of the right ventricle. This artery is a division point between the mediastinum and the two branches that travel to the lungs.

red blood cells: cells without a nucleus that transport oxygen to tissues of the body.

right atrium: the area that the blue blood enters first that makes up the upper chamber, right portion of the heat.

right ventricle: this ventricle is the portion of the heart that pumps blood into the lungs and through the pulmonary arteries.

sanguirenal: the blood which is supplied to the kidneys.

spleen: this organ functions to remove and destroy dead blood cells from the blood stream.

stethoscope: a tool used to amplify the sounds of the heart and lungs.

systolic: the distinct period of the cardiac cycle when pressure of the artery walls is highest, resulting in the number given that is of a higher amount in the measurement of the blood pressure.

tachycardia: the description of rapid heart contractions in the heart's rhythm.

thrombocytes: used to refer to blood platelets.

thrombus: used to describe a blood clot.

Tricuspid valve: the blood leaves the right atrium to pass through this valve on its way to the right ventricle.

varicose: the condition that describes the distension of the veins.

vena cava: the inferior and the superior vein which is responsible for transporting the used blood to the heart.

ventricles: the lower, larger portions of the heart.

ventricular septal defect: a congenital cardiac anomaly or defect that occurs.

venules: passageways that return blood from tissues to veins to be returned to the heart.

vessel: a structure for carrying fluid (like blood).

Respiratory System

Respiratory System Process

The air enters the nose through the nostrils or nares. The air that enters is filtered by tiny filaments or hairs known as cilia in the nose. The mucous membranes work to warm and moisten the air that passes to the back of the throat or pharynx. The air travels to the windpipe or trachea. A flap made from cartilage opens and closes at the top of the windpipe. This flap is called an epiglottis and works to keep food out of the airway passage. Inside the windpipe, you will find a voice box. This voice box is also referred to as the larynx. The larynx is protected by thyroid cartilage which is simply a protrusion of the Adam's apple. The windpipe has two pathways that break off from each other shortly after that point. These two pathways divided into the right bronchi and the left bronchi.

The air moves into the bronchi pathways to the smaller divisions called bronchioles. Inside the lung are found the smallest of all the air sacs. These sacs are called alveoli. The lungs are in the thorax or in the chest cavity. This is also known as the thoracic cavity. The thoracic cavity is enclosed by the sternum and the diaphragm. The more tapered of the two lungs has two lobes. This tapered lung can be found in the left quadrant of the thoracic cavity. The pulmonary artery flows from the right ventricle into the lungs. This allows the lungs to carry on the process of oxygenation of the blood. The blood's hemoglobin absorbs the oxygen and carries to all parts of the body. Excessive carbon dioxide in the blood causes the brain to increase breathing rates and therefore allows this process of blood oxygenation to increase and oxygen can be improved.

Review Video: Respiratory System
Visit mometrix.com/academy and enter code: 783075

Respiratory System Terms

adenoids: the lymphatic tissue which can be found in the nasopharynx or throat within the body.

alveoli: the air sacs located within the lungs.

anoxia: the condition that results from an absence of oxygen.

anthracosis: the disease that is a result of breathing in toxic levels of coal dust.

asbestosis: the disease that is a result of breathing in toxic levels of asbestos.

bronchi: the term given to describe the two tubes dividing or separating the trachea.

capillaries: blood vessels that are small in size.

carbon dioxide: the product or outcome of the process of respiration.

chalicosis: a disease which is the result of the inhalation of the dust or sand into the lungs.

ciliated: projections that have hair like qualities and appearance.

dyspnea: a term used to describe when a person has a hard time breathing.

eupnea: the term given when breathing is on a normal scale.

larynx: the voice box or organ responsible for speech.

mediastinum: the interpleural space or gap.

osmosis: the process that occurs when a substance passes through a porous or absorbent membrane.

pharynx: the passageway known as the throat.

phrenic: having to do with the diaphragm.

phrenoplegia: the term given to describe the condition of paralysis or immobility of the diaphragm.

pleura: the moist membrane which covers or lines the lungs.

pleurisy: the condition in which is indicative of an inflammation within the pleura or lining in the lungs.

pneumocentesis: the term given when a surgical procedure punctures the lungs to drain fluid.

pneumonia: the term given to describe an acute or severe inflammation of the lungs.

pneumothorax: the condition that describes a collection of air in the pleural cavity of the body that leads to lung collapse.

rales: this describes an abnormal rattling sound heard on auscultation of the lungs.

saccule: the term given to describe a small sack found within the lungs.

septum: the wall or lining that separates the nostrils in the nose.

stethemia: the term given to describe congestion within the lungs.

thorax: the upper body between the diaphragm and neck, referred to as the chest area.

thyroid cartilage: also referred to as the Adam's apple which is a protrusion of cartilage.

trachea: a tube or passageway that comes from the larynx and extends to the bronchi.

Digestive System

Digestive System Process

Salivation allows our food to mix with the saliva in order to form a bolus. The term bolus refers to the round shape of food that is formed within our mouths through chewing or mastication. This shape or bolus allows us to swallow or deglutition more easily. The food is then blocked by the epiglottis from entering the airway. The epiglottis is a barrier or flap made from a cartilaginous substance. The passageway that carries the food to the stomach is known as the esophagus. A chemical process occurs within the stomach. A lining in the abdominal cavity is called the peritoneum. The chemicals involved in this process are hydrochloric acid and enzymes. Gastric juices within the stomach are acidic. The chemicals work together to dissolve the bolus into a liquid form that can be easily transported through the intestines. The liquid form of the bolus is referred to as the chyme.

The matter or contents inside the stomach are then transported through the small intestine by way of the pyloric valve or the sphincter. Swells of involuntary contractions within the digestive tract are known as peristalsis. The colon is divided into sections. Inside these sections, you will find tiny hairs called villi. The first section of the small intestine of the colon is the duodenum. The bile released into the duodenum is transported from the gallbladder. The duodenum is followed by the jejunum. The final section of the small intestine is the ileum. The large intestine opens at the ileocecal valve at the end of the small intestine. The large intestine of the colon is shaped in an s-curve. This portion that is shaped in an s-curve is known as the sigmoid. The rectum is closed off by the sphincter muscles known as the anus.

Review Video: Gastrointestinal System
Visit mometrix.com/academy and enter code: 378740

Digestive System Terms

ase: enzyme.

bucc: cheek.

celio: abdomen.

deciduous: the name that is used to refer to a person's baby teeth.

dent: teeth.

diverticulitis: a hereditary disease of the colon that can restrict a person's dietary habits.

edentulous: without teeth.

enterocolitis: the painful, presence of inflammation within the small intestine and the colon.

esophagus: the tube or passageway joining the throat to the stomach.

Eustachian tube: the canal or passageway that links the pharynx or throat to the middle ear.

gastroduodenitis: the painful, presence of inflammation within the stomach and the duodenum.

gingiv: gum

gingivitis: the presence of a painful inflammation within the gums of the mouth.

glyc(o): sweetness; glucose

hepat: liver.

ileum: the lower end or section of the small intestine.

jejunum: the secondary section of the small intestine that joins the duodenum.

labio: lip.

lingua: tongue.

mesentery: a fold or crease within the peritoneum that links the intestine to the posterior abdominal wall.

molars: the term given to refer to a person's back teeth.

peristalsis: this is the term given to the wavelike contractions which occur in the small intestine. These contractions are responsible for helping the food to be moved down the intestine for disposal.

ptyalin: a digestive component which is found in the substance known as saliva.

pylorectomy: the term given when the pylorus is removed by a surgical procedure.

pyloric valve: the valve or regulator that allows food to leave the stomach.

pyorrhea: discharge of pus; inflamed tissue around the teeth

salivary glands: glands responsible for the salivation process found within the mouth.

stoma: mouth.

Genitourinary System

amenorrhea: the word used to refer to the condition where a female does not have a menstrual period.

andro: male.

anthropo: human race.

areola: the term used to describe the portion surrounding the nipple on the breast.

carnal knowledge: the term given for the act of sexual intercourse.

cerv: neck.

cervix: this is the opening of the uterus found in the female.

circumcision: the surgical removal of the foreskin on a male's organ.

clitoris: the female erectile organ that is stimulated during sexual intercourse.

colpo: vagina.

copulation: the term given for the act of sexual intercourse.

crypt: hidden.

D&C: a procedure that results in the dilatation and curettage of the female organs.

dysmenorrheal: a persistent and extremely painful menstruation period.

ectopic: the word used to describe the condition that exists when an organ is not in its normal setting.

endometrium: the word given to refer to the lining of membrane found in the uterus.

enuresis: the accidental and involuntary emptying of the contents within the bladder.

episiotomy: the enlargement of the vulval orifice accomplished through a surgical procedure which is often performed for child birth.

fallopian: the word used to refer to tubes that carry the eggs to the uterus.

fraternal twins: two eggs joined to become two babies.

graafian follicles: the tiny, microscopic sacs located within the ovaries of the female.

gravid: the word used to describe the condition of pregnancy.

hydro: water.

hymen: the word used to refer to the lining or membrane found at the mouth of the vagina.

hysterectomy: the operation that results in the removal of the uterus from the female.

incontinence: the term given to describe an involuntary emptying of the bladder.

inguinal: the word used to describe parts that have to do with the groin.

intravenous pyelogram: a procedure involving dye and x-rays of the pelvic region that highlights function and anatomy of the urinary system.

litmus paper: the material used to help decide whether or not a urine sample is of an acidic base or an alkaline base.

mastectomy: the operation that results in the removal of the breast.

metr: uterus.

micturition: also known as the process of urination.

nephron: the operative unit of the kidney.

nullipara: this term is given to a woman who has remained childless.

oophorectomy: the surgical operation that results in the removal of an ovary.

oophoro: ovary.

orch: testicle.

orchis: the term used to refer to the testicle in the male species.

orchitis: the word used to refer to a condition of painful, inflammation of the testes.

oviduct: the term given to refer to the fallopian tube.

parturition: the word used to describe the time period and process that is undergone during child birth.

postpartum: the term given to describe the time after a woman gives birth.

prepuce: the word used to refer to foreskin.

prostate: this refers to the gland in a man that is positioned around the urethra that can affect and restrict the flow of urine when inflammation is present.

retroversion: the word to refer to the flip-flop placement of the uterus in the wrong location.

salpingitis: the term given when an inflammation is present within the fallopian tubes.

salpingo: tube.

scrotum: the sac on the male body that contains the male's testicles.

sterility: the word to describe a person's inability of reproduction.

ureters: the tubes that extend from the organs known as the kidneys.

urethra: this passageway or tube extends out from the bladder.

vulva: the word used to refer to female genitalia.

Nervous System

acrophobia: an extreme fear of high places.

ambi: neutral or both sides.

analgesic: a medication that takes away the pain.

aphasia: the term given to describe the loss of verbal expression.

arachnoid: part of the meninges between the dura mater and the pia mater.

arborization: a tree like pattern with branches such as that of a nerve fiber.

auto: self.

bi: two.

blephar: eyelid.

caudal: a term used to refer to the rear or tail.

cerebrospinal fluid: the liquid that cushions the brain and spinal cord within a protective layer.

cerebrum: the term used to refer to the biggest and uppermost portion of the brain.

claustrophobia: an extreme fear of closed in places.

coma: the term given to refer to a period of unresponsiveness.

craniotomy: an operation that opens the skull by surgical means.

cyclo: circle or cycle.

delusion: a term that refers to a bogus belief.

derm: skin.

di: two.

e, ex: out.

efferent: the term given to the nerves that carry impulses or messages from the brain.

encephalon: a term used to refer to the brain.

eu: normal or good.

ganglion: the term given to describe a set or gathering of nerve cells into a knot formation.

hallucination: the term given to describe a misconception of a sensory impression.

hemi: half.

hemiplegia: the term given to describe the immobility or paralysis that effects one side of the body.

hydrocephalus: a buildup of cerebrospinal fluid upon the brain.

itis: inflammation.

kine: movement.

kinetic: having to do with movement.

kleptomania: the uncontrollable urge to steal.

lacri: tears.

macrocephaly: the condition of having an unusually, big head.

medulla oblongata: the portion of the brain responsible for the functions of breathing and heart rates within the body.

meninges: membranes that cover the brain or spinal cord.

meningitis: the present of inflammation within the lining of the brain or spinal cord.

myelitis: the term given to describe spinal cord inflammation.

neuralgia: pain caused by inflammation or damage to a nerve.

neuron: the term that refers to a nerve cell.

ocul: eye.

oto: ear.

paresis: a term used to refer to a state of partial palalysis or immobility.

paroxysm: the term given when a person experiences a spasm or contracted muscle.

peripheral: a term used to refer to a position of outer boundary or furthest from the center.

phobia: unusual or unwarranted fear.

photo: light.

phren: mind.

plegia: paralysis or immobility.

plexus: a term used to refer to a complex arrangement of nerves.

psychic: the term given to indicate a mental ability.

pyromania: the unnatural obsession with fire and objects that cause fire.

schizophrenia: a term used to describe a serious, mental disorder.

sciatic nerve: a nerve located in the hip.

scler: hard.

syncope: a term used to refer to the act of fainting or passing out.

tic: a term used to refer to an involuntary twinge.

ventricle: a term that refers to a slight cavity or hollow.

vertigo: a condition of light headedness or dizziness.

voluntary: muscles that are used to write or type are categorized as this type.

The Senses

cornea: the transparent portion of the sclera.

fenestra vestibuli: this refers to the oval window.

iris: the muscular layer enclosing the pupil in which the coloration exists.

lacrimal: having to do with tears.

lens: translucent biconvex body within the eye or visual organ.

myopia: the condition that is also referred to as nearsightedness.

nystagmus: the action that refers to the involuntary movement that results in the jerking of the eye.

ossicle: a small bone.

sclera: the white portion of the eye.

tympanic membrane: the organ that is referred to as the eardrum.

Process of Hearing Sounds

The organs responsible for hearing are the ears. Ears hear by translations of the vibrations that are transformed into the sounds that we hear. The outer ear is known as pinna. The pinna is responsible for collecting the sound waves that vibrate. The vibrations move down towards the external auditory canal or meatus. The end point of the external auditory canal is known as the tympanic membrane or eardrum. There are three small bones inside the middle ear known as ossicles. The hammer, the anvil, and the stirrup are the three bones. The hammer is also known by its Latin name as malleus. The anvil's Latin name is incus. The stirrup's Latin name is stapes. The Eustachian tube links the middle to the pharynx. The air pressure is maintained and equalized by this tube in relationship to the atmospheric pressure.

Inner Ear

The inner ear has a spiral shaped tunnel known as the cochlea. The cochlea is known to contain the sensory ends of the auditory nerve. The cochlea is responsible for true hearing. The mechanism responsible for maintaining a person's equilibrium is also found in the inner ear. Equilibrium allows us to keep our balance. Many inner ear problems cause vertigo or dizziness. These problems may be worsened when infection or imbalances occur within the inner ear. Vertigo may require the treatment from a doctor. Occasionally, there may be a ringing in the ears. This ringing in the ears is called tinnitus. Tinnitus is not uncommon in persons who have suffered nerve damage to the ears. Earaches or otalgia should be treated to prevent damage of this type to the ear. Hearing can be impacted negatively when these conditions are left untreated or treated improperly.

Eyes

The eyes are responsible for seeing. The eyeball has a protection in the form of an orbital socket in the skull. The eyeball's movements are accomplished by the muscles in this area. The three layers of the eyeball are the sclera, the choroid, and the retina. They all have different functions. The sclera is found in the outer part of the eyeball. The sclera is a durable layer. The next layer is sandwich between the sclera and the retina. It is the vascular layer. The vascular layer has blood vessels and is referred to as the choroid. The retina functions to allow the images that are seen to be focused. The macula lutea is the point in which the vision has the most clarity. The light rays may be focused in front of the retina making the person nearsighted. Nearsightedness is also known as the condition of myopia.

The light rays may be focused in back of the retina causing the person to have hyperopia. The transparent front portion of the sclera is known as the cornea. It is in the cornea that light rays enter the eye. Either of these conditions may require glasses or corrective surgery techniques. A licensed physician can help make these determinations. The mucous membrane covering the front of the eyeball is known as the conjunctiva. Occasionally, the eye may suffer from an increase intraocular pressure which is also known as glaucoma. Glaucoma is more common in the elderly. There are other conditions which can have a negative impact on vision. Diplopia or double vision may occur. Inflammation of the eyelid or blepharitis may also occur. Dim vision or amblyopia is also a problem that can affect a person's vision for the worse.

Eye Terms

caput: head.

cataract: a condition that makes the lens clouded and unclear.

choroid: the vascular layer found in the eye.

conjunctivitis: the condition in which an inflammation exists in the membrane located in the front of the eye.

contra: against.

corium: true or genuine skin.

corpus: body.

diplopia: the term given to seeing double.

follicle: the area in which a root of hair is embedded or set in.

glaucoma: a term used to refer to an opacity of the lens in the eye.

glossitis: a term to refer to the condition of swelling and inflammation of the tongue

infra: under.

inter: between.

Iris sphincter: the muscle located in the eye which causes the pupil to constrict.

lacrimal sac: dacryocyst.

lens: the crystalline structure found in the eyes.

locus: place.

melanin: the substance that creates the skin pigmentation or color.

novo: new.

nul: no.

olfactory: having to do with the senses that allow for smell.

ophthalmologist: a specialized doctor that can diagnosis and treat eye disease.

optician: the licensed expert that has the ability to fill a prescription for eyewear.

optometrist: a licensed professional who can provide sight testing and correction.

otitis media: the condition in which the middle ear has an infection.

papillae: the elevations or bumps on the tongue which contain the taste buds.

per diem: by the day.

pro: for.

sebaceous glands: the glands found in the skin that produce oil.

Snellen chart: the test that is given to measure visual acuity.

strabismus: a severe deviation of the eyes.

sudoriferous glands: another term for sweat glands.

tinnitus: the name of the condition in which a ringing in the ears exists.

Latin Legal Vocabulary

a fortiori: by the stronger reason.

a priori: deductive.

ab initio: from the beginning.

ad hoc: in the light of day.

ad infinitum: without limit.

ad interim: in the meantime.

ad litem: pending the suit.

ad valorem: according to value.

animo: with intent.

antenuptial: before a marriage.

arguendo: for the sake of argument.

bipartite: in two parts.

casus fortuitus: unforeseen occurrence.

casus: event.

compos mentis: sane.

contra: against.

corpus delicti: the body of the crime.

corpus: the body.

cum testamento annexo: with the will annexed.

de bene esse: of temporary validity

de facto: actual.

de jure: by right.

de novo: over again.

delicto: wrong.

duces tecum: bring with you.

et ux.: and wife.

et. al.: and others.

gravamen: the gist or general idea.

habeas corpus: writ for speedy release.

ibidem (ibid.): same.

id est: that is.

imprimatur: sanction or endorse.

in absentia: in absence or nonattendance.

in causa mortis: at the point or brink of death.

in extremis: near death.

in flagrante delicto: in the act of committing the offense.

in limine: preliminary.

in loco parentis: in the place of a parent.

in medias res: into the middle of the matter.

in propria persona: in ones's own behalf.

in rem: opposed to or against the thing.

in toto: wholly.

incorporeal: intangible.

infra: beneath.

inter alia: among other things.

inter vivos: between living persons.

intra vires: in conclusion.

ipse: he, himself.

ipso facto: by the fact or act itself.

lex loci: law of the place.

lex non scripta: unwritten law.

lex terrae: a law of the land.

mala fides: bad faith.

mala in se: acts which are morally wrong.

mea culpea: "I did it".

mens rea: guilty mind.

modicum: a small amount.

modus operandi: method of procedure.

modus: manner.

nisi: unless.

non compos mentis: not of sound mind.

non sequitur: it does not follow.

nudum pactum: bare contract.

obiter dictum: said in passing.

pactum: agreement.

pari delicto: equal fault.

pari passu: same grade.

per curiam: by the court.

prima facie: on the first view.

pro bono publico: for the public good.

pro rata: proportionately.

pro tempore: for the time being.

pro tempore: temporarily.

pro: singularly.

quantum meruit: as much as he deserves.

quid pro quo: something for something.

res ipsa loquitur: the thing speaks for itself.

res judicata: already judicially decided.

res: thing.

scienter: knowledge.

scilicet: to wit.

scintilla: slightest.

sine qua non: something that is essential.

sotto voce: whispered.

sui generis: unique.

Criminal Vocabulary

abettor: a person who persuades another to commit a crime.

abscond: to hide or leave the region in an attempt to avoid punishment or trial.

absolve: to release or not hold a person to a responsibility.

accessory after the fact: a person who hides a criminal from the law.

accessory before the fact: a person who devises the planned steps for a bank robbery.

acquittal: a discharge of a verdict of guilt by a jury after a trial has been carried out.

alias: a fictitious name that is given in place of a person's birth or legal name.

animus furandi: to have the intention to steal or rob someone.

bail: the security that an accused person puts up to secure release before the trial is held.

battery: to illegally touch someone in order to do them harm.

bribe: a gift, promise, or favor that is offered in an effort to get someone else to carry out an unlawful action.

collusion: a secretive agreement that is meant to defraud someone else.

confiscation: the act of the state in taking a property of a person who has committed a crime.

confrontation: placing the witness and the defendant in face to face positions.

constructive breaking: to break and enter into an establishment or home through means of fraud.

contempt: the willful disobedience or disrespect given to the judge or court.

contraband: the name given to refer to property that is illegal to have in your possession.

corporeal: tangible or substantial.

corroborate: to strengthen or reflect a sense of truth or credibleness.

culpable: guilty of wrongdoing.

embezzle: to appropriate or take someone else's property when they have entrusted into your care.

exculpate: to clear from blame of all wrongdoing.

exemplar: fingerprints or other means by which identification can be verified.

exonerate: to free or release a person from a charge.

extradition: the delivery of the person to be tried or punished to either another state or another country.

forgery: to alter a document or writing in an effort to defraud someone.

incarcerate: the act of putting someone in prison or behind bars.

indictment: a charge or accusation by a grand jury.

manslaughter: the killing of another person without thought of premeditated intent or malice.

mea culp: the act of stating that you are guilty of the wrongdoing.

parole: let go or release of a convicted person before the end of the term or length of the sentence charged.

preliminary: a hearing or procedure that is held in order to decide whether or not the prosecution has enough evidence in which to warrant a trial of the person charged with the crime.

reprieve: a postponement until a later date of the punishment that has been decided upon.

robbery: to take someone's property from a violent or forceful act.

"third degree": to give someone an extended period of questioning in a threatening manner.

utter: to offer a forged or fake document.

Torts

absolute liability: liability or responsibility without holding a person at fault.

action in rem: action against a thing.

allegation: statements given in the form of factual information that are used to prove a point.

assumption of risk: the responsibility falls upon the person injured when the accident occurred due to the person's ignoring of the warning signs.

attractive nuisance: an unguarded and alluring situation that could tempt someone to venture forth into an unsafe situation.

bona fide: in good faith.

bringing a lawsuit as an indigent: also referred as "in forma pauperis".

chattels: the private or personal property of someone.

constructive notice: the existence of a dangerous situation long before the actual accident occurs.

contributory negligence: a want of care or caution on the part of the person who is making the complaint.

damnum absque injuria: an injury upon which there is no way to make a recovery from a decision made by the courts or judge.

efficient intervening cause: a situation in which the defendant is negligent, but the plaintiff is unable to gain recovery or recompense.

exemplary damages: damages or costs that are above the actual damages incurred.

Good Samaritan Statue: a law that protects a person from being sued when they have committed an act of giving emergency assistance.

imputation of negligence: placing the responsibility of another person's act of negligence upon the shoulders of another.

judgement: the final determination of a court regarding a person's guilt or legal responsibility.

last clear chance: a situation in which the defendant may be proven negligent but still claims a lack of responsibility out of the circumstances in which the plaintiff could have avoided the situation n the end.

libel: defamation by a writing or publication.

licensee: a person who enters another's property with the consent of the owner.

mental anguish: the suffering and anxiety that a person goes through due to an event that has caused that person emotional stress and hardship.

mitigation: abatement or alleviation.

nominal damages: a small or trifling sum of money.

nonfeasance: a charge resulting in a person's lack of action.

prima facie: verbal or oral defamation.

proximate cause: the cause of an event or happening.

punitive damages: damages or costs that a defendant receives.

real or actual damages: tangible or visible damages or costs.

redress: satisfaction for an injury that has been incurred.

res ipsa loquitur: the thing speaks for itself.

respondeat superior: doctrine that holds the employer as liable or responsible.

slander: oral or verbal defamation.

tortfeasor: one who is negligent of their responsibility.

trespasser: a person who illegally enters or steps onto another person's property.

trial de novo: a new trial of a court case.

vendor: seller of property.

wrongful act: torturous activity that brings harm.

Contracts

acquiescence: a silent agreement.

ancillary: auxillary.

assignable: the ability to transfer.

breach of contract: failure to reach the agreed upon ending results of the terms established in the contract.

carte blanche: to be able to have full reign without restrictions.

caveat emptor: let the buyer beware.

coercion: constraint placed upon someone else.

collateral: an indirect assurance of another debt.

compensatory damages: the costs given in order to compensate the injured party.

competent parties: persons who have the ability to hold the responsibility of making a legal contractual agreement.

counteroffer: changes or alterations made in an offer received.

escalator clause: a clause or legality that states that the payments can be changed if the conditions exist to warrant such a change.

ex contractu: arising from a contractual agreement.

executory: a contract with something that has not been performed by one or both parties involved.

express warranty: the guarantee from a manufacturer that the product purchased will perfom in the manner that has been promised.

express: a verbal or oral contractual agreement.

forbearance: a promise to not proceed with an action.

gratuitous promise: an agreement in which no valuables or consideration is expected to be paid.

implied: a contract with no actual promise spelled out in verbal communications.

inchoate: incomplete.

insolvency: the inability to pay the debts that have been incurred.

meritorious consideration: the promise of monetary funds to a charity in a specific amount.

mistake: a contractual term that means that the parties involved could not come up with an agreement that meets both parties demands.

nudum pactum: a contractual agreement that has been made without consideration.

offer: tender.

pactum: agreement.

parol: oral or verbal.

performance: the fulfillment of the agreed upon terms of the contractual agreement.

privity of contract: the relationship of the persons involved in the contractual agreement.

pro tanto: as far as it goes.

uantum meruit: as much as he deserves or has earned.

quid pro quo: consideration.

seal: a sign or stamp that gives the instrument in question a certain air of authenticity.

Statue of Frauds: the document which clearly expresses what types of contracts must be made in a written form.

subrogation: taking the place of the person who originally made the contractual agreement.

surety: a person that is agreeable to be the stand in for another person's debt or obligations.

to abrogate: to annul or repeal a matter.

to alienate: to transfer.

to put into effect: execute.

unilateral: a contract in which the act has reached a satisfactory note of acceptance.

usury: the greatest amount of interest that is permitted to be charged in accordance with the law.

vitiate: to destroy the legality of the contractual agreement.

Real Property

abstract: the history of the previous person's that have held title to a real property.

affinity: a relationship with the blood kin of a husband or wife.

alimony pendent elite: the monies paid for alimony when a divorce has not been finalized.

antenupial: the term that means "before marriage".

appurtenance: something which is attached to the land indefinitely and permanently.

basis for granting divorce: the grounds or circumstances that warrant a divorce.

bigamy: a marriage in which there are two wives or two husbands in existence during the same period of time.

cloud on title: an impairment of the title.

cohabitation: living in a relationship as husband and wife.

collusion: an agreement in which brings about a fabrication of false evidence.

common-law marriage: a marriage that has been entered in upon mutual agreement without ceremony.

community property: the property that a married couple has obtained during the course of the marriage.

conciliation: to come to an agreed upon settlement without animosity.

condonation: a pardon or forgiving of an offense.

conjugal: marriage.

consanguinity: the blood kin relationship.

consortium: conjugal or wedded fellowship of husband and wife.

convey: to transfer property to another owner.

coverture: a woman that is married.

defeasible title: a title that can be avoided or ignored.

domicile: the legal residence in which you live.

easement: the legal right that gives a person to use another person's land.

eminent domain: the legal right of the governmental authorities to buy up private property for public use.

enceinte: with child or pregnant.

Enoch Arden: a law that gives grounds for obtaining a divorce based on the continuous absence of the party in question.

fee simple: unconditional ownership of the land without any questions.

femme sole: a woman who is unmarried.

fixture: the chattel that has been attached to a real property or holding.

homestead: a place in which a family lives that has been protected by law from creditors

hypothecate: to promise or pledge without actually delivering a title.

lien: the legal claim on property in order to gain settlement of a debt that is owed.

mensa et thoro: a separation during the marriage.

metes and bounds: the boundaries and corners which denote the physical measurements of a piece of property.

miscegenation: a marriage in which the parties are not of the same racial ethnicity.

monogamy: a marriage in which there is only one man and one woman involved in the relationship.

necessaries: the food, clothing, housing, and medical costs that are needed to sustain a quality of life.

no-fault divorce: a provision or law that states that the person filing for the divorce does not have to find or prove that their marital partner is at fault.

party wall: a wall that has been put up on the property line that is shared by both parties.

plat: the map that lays out the division of land into lots or sections.

premarital: a promise or agreement made before the actual marriage ceremony.

prescription: gaining a title by an extended period of use of the property.

property settlement: the agreed upon disposition of the community property of the married parties.

public domain: governmental ownership of a piece of property.

quitclaim deed: a document that state's or conveys the interest and limits of those of the person who owns the document.

redemption: purchasing back property that has been foreclosed upon.

right of survivorship: joint tenancy.

riparian owner: the person who has ownership over the land that joins the waterway.

seisin: the actual possession or custody of the property.

sequestration: the taking of property to gain custody over it.

vinculo matrimonii: the term that means divorce in the Latin language.

voidable marriage: the term given for a marriage that could be voided or negated.

warranty deed: a deed or document which gives the buyer a vested title to the property.

Probate and Wills

abatement: the decrease or lessening of an inheritance or legacy due to a lack of funds.

ademption: the withdrawal of a legacy or inheritance.

administrator: the person a court appoints to be responsible for an estate.

ambulatory: an instrument or document that is able to be changed or altered in some way.

animus revocandi: intent to revoke.

attest: to bear witness to.

attestation clause: clause or legal statement that witnesses verify that the will was executed in proper order.

causa mortis: in anticipation of a death that is close at hand.

cestui que trust: beneficiary of a trust.

chattel: anything that consists of the personal property.

codicil: modification or alteration of a will.

cognomen: a family name shared by relatives.

consanguinity: blood kin.

conservator: an individual that incapacitated in some way has this person to manage their properties.

cum testamento annexo: with the will annexed.

cy-press doctrine: the court's effort to carry out the intent and wishes of the testator in meeting the terms of the will.

de facto: accepted for practical reasons and purposes.

devise: to bequeath.

escheat: the state's acquirement of a property through reversion.

executor: the person given instructions to follow in accordance with the wishes of the testator of the will.

guardian ad litem: a person who has been designated or assigned by the court to represent a minor in a litigation.

hereditatments: inherited property or property subject to be inherited.

holographic: the handwritten document that is known as the will.

indefeasible: something that can hold up and not be voided or negated.

legacy: a bequest or inheritance.

legatee: a person who receives a bequest or an inheritance in a will.

nuncupative: an oral or verbalized will is known as this term.

per stripes: for representation.

precatory: words that are expressed as a desire or wish.

pretermitted: a heir that was accidentally omitted.

prima facie: at first sight.

primogeniture: the condition which meets the circumstances of being the first born.

probate: a legal, court procedure that proves the validity of a will.

putative: supposed.

remainderman: the person that is entitled to an estate after the rights of a precedent estate have expired or ended.

republication: the re-execution of a will that was in existence prior to the marriage.

residuary estate: what is left after the estate has had the expenses, debts, and bequests settled.

revoke: to cancel or rescind an agreement.

testatrix: the woman that scribes her own will.

ward: a person who is usually underage that has a legal guardian.

Agency, Corporations, Negotiable Instruments

affirms the decision: this happens when an appellate court decides in agreement with the decision upon which a lower court has made.

agent: a person that has the legal authority to carry out the business of another person.

agreement: covenant or promise made.

attachment: the legal custody or collection of property.

Bill of Rights: The first 10 amendments to the Constitution make up this document.

binder: a temporary insurance provided to meet risks due to special circumstances that may occur.

blue-sky laws: laws in existence to protect persons from investing in corporations of a fraudulent nature.

board of directors: the managing and governing of a corporation is carried out by this unit of people.

bona fide: the absence of fraud or unfair dealings or practices.

but without proof: alleged crimes that are stated.

by the day: per diem.

bylaws: rules that guide the management and operation of a corporation.

capital stock: the financial basis that forms the foundation of the corporation.

capital: the corporation's assets.

carrier: the transporter or shipper of the goods or freight sold.

certiorari: the sending of a cause from a lower court to a superior court in the judicial system.

charter: the document that the corporation gains the authority to act.

citation: reference to a precedent set.

collateral acceptance: an accepted agreement that is made in writing referring to a valuable that is not the negotiable instrument being purchased.

commercial paper: negotiable instruments or documents.

commingle: to mix or combine a fiduciary's funds with a client's funds.

common stock: dividends fluctuate with the corporation's earnings and profits.

consideration: quid pro quo.

covenant: agreement or promise.

cross-examination: the redirect examination follows this questioning.

cruel and unusual punishment: the Eight Amendment of the Constitution prevents persons from receiving this inhumane treatment.

de jure dissolution: a dissolution that has been made because of a judicial decree.

debenture: a note or bond that has the funding backed by the credit in which the corporation can obtain or holds.

default: the happening in which a defendant does not answer in a civil proceeding.

defendant: a person that has a motion or request for a judgment to be made by the court.

demand note: a payment that must be paid when requested.

dishonor: the failure to pay the debt as agreed.

dissolution: termination or end of a corporation.

double jeopardy: The Fifth Amendment of the Constitution prohibits a person from being tried twice for the same crime.

drawee: the person accepting the negotiable instrument.

endorsement in blank: gives the person who holds the instrument the right to receive payment.

excusing a prospective juror for cause: a stated or apparent reason that gives the attorney reason to dismiss a prospective juror from a case.

freedom of religion: The First Amendment of the Constitution gives this right to American citizens.

freedom of speech: The First Amendment of the Constitution provides this right to the American people.

general agent: the authorized person who can transact business.

holder: the person who the negotiable instrument has been delivered or distributed.

implied agency: an agency created out of particular actions of parties involved in a situation.

imprisonment: incarceration or loss of freedom.

in camera: in chambers.

independent contractor: a worker in which the agency has little or no control.

indictment: accusation of the crime by the grand jury.

issues in a lawsuit: the points or areas of disagreement within the lawsuit.

kiting checks: checks written without the funds on hand.

Laches: a doctrine that states that rights that have been neglected over a period of time are not enforceable.

legal opinion: an authoritative interpretation of a stature or law.

liquidation: the final winding up of all corporate affairs in an effort to change properties into a cash flow.

M'Naghten rule: the laws that allow for the defendant to plead and be found insane.

maturity: the date that a note or instrument comes up as due and payable.

merger: an absorption of one company into another.

mutual consent: the like mindedness of people.

naked: incomplete or unfinished.

nominal: not substantial or significant.

note: a written agreement or promise to make payment.

original jurisdiction: the court in which first adjudicated or tried the lawsuit.

par: nominal face value of a share.

partnership: a business that is shared by two people who take responsibility for the profits or losses that the business incurs.

pass for cause: this term is applied when the attorney dismisses a juror for no apparent reason of a stated prejudice.

perpetual succession: the corporation exists in a state of change regarding its membership that has no effect upon the corporation's continuation.

plea of nolo contendere: a statement that says, "I do not wish to contest the charge."

plenipotentiary: the person given full authority to run the business.

plenipotentiary: the person who holds the power necessary to transact business for a firm.

power: the right to do something.

preclusion: estoppel.

preferred stock: the stock or unit of share that receives prioritized payments when dividends are paid out.

presentment: the presentation of a note or demand for payment.

principal: caveat emptor.

private: a corporation that is run by individuals without governmental powers or functions.

pro se: in propria persona.

promoter: the person that forms the corporation.

proprietor: the owner of the business.

protest: a statement or declaration before a notary because of a nonpayment.

proxy: the vote that has been authorized by another individual in his stead.

public: a corporation formed for political reasons.

quorum: the number of members that must be present to conduct a transaction for the business.

reading back to the jury: to read back the information given during the hearing while simultaneously omitting any questions that have received an objection and have been sustained by the judge.

receiver: the court appointed person that acts on behalf of the business concerns of the corporation.

revocation: the recall of something previously granted or given.

right: the authority given to act.

scope of his authority: the knowledge of the agent is imputed to be knowledge shared by the principal.

seal: a symbol that gives a certain air of authenticity to an instrument or document.

share: the unit or portion that gives the holder a part ownership in the company.

silent partner: the person that stays in the background to avoid public recognition in a company.

special agent: an agent working to perform a single transaction.

special endorsement: an endorsement or backing that specifies who receives the payment from an instrument or share.

stare decisis: the principle that is considered when the court follows the precedents of law held in prior courts.

time note: an agreement that has the documented specific date that the payment should be made.

to contest in law: litigation or trial in a court of law.

to profess: to purport or claim.

treasury stock: stock that is owned by a corporation and sold by that same corporation in legitimate transactions.

ultra vires: beyond the powers.

venue: geographical jurisdiction of the authorities.

Depositions

a solemn penalty for perjury: affirmation.

appearance fee: per diem.

caption: name and number of the case and court where it was filed.

jurat: a certificate of a person that a writing was sworn under.

provisionally: de bene esse.

subpoena: a command that a person be in attendance to a procedure or hearing.

Technology

Americans With Disabilities Act: the law which mandates that equal access to courtrooms and public facilities be available to all Americans regardless of their disabilities.

atlas: satellite.

backup file: a file that duplicates or is used to copy the master file for security reasons

binary digit: bit or unit of measurement in the computer's storage.

boot: to start up the computer.

burster: a machine that separates fanfold paper into single sheets of paper.

byte: a unit of storage equal to eight bits.

captioning: real-time feed of the reporter is integrated into the television's program to enable a person to view the words being spoken aloud.

computer-integrated courtroom: a computer system that allows the judge, the lawyers, and other court participants the opportunity to view the reporter's real-time feed.

conflict: a steno outline that has more than one English translation within its body.

Court Reporters Forum: a gathering of reporters on CompuServe.

default value: the value that the computer sets automatically.

DOS: disk operating system found in the computer.

dump: the transferring of information into another system.

glitch: an anomaly or problem within the computer.

global: a correction that is applicable for the entire work performed.

hard copy: the term used to refer to the paper formatted version of the work.

imaging: a scanning of an image or photograph that does not produce ASCII readable text.

Internet: a network of computers that link together.

keyword index: particular words or phrases noted within the transcript have been formatted into this list.

kilobyte (kB): unit of storage equal to 1024 bytes of storage found on the computer.

LEXIS: computer assisted legal research system.

litigation support software: real-time, current testimony is presented on the monitors of the lawyers and judges while the professional searches and organizes other information.

matrix printer: a machine that prints out in characters composed of dots.

megabyte: the unit of storage that is equivalent to 1,000,000 bytes.

menu: list of functions that the computer performs.

merging: formulating two files into one single file.

modem: telecommunication device used for communication with the use of computers.

optical character recognition: the production of an ASCII readable text.

port: a location for connecting a wire or device to a piece of hardware.

random access memory: RAM.

real-time: instant translation of outlines into the English language.

rough draft: an ASCII file that has unedited testimony in its conclusion.

scanning: the mechanical device that allows for the transference of a data to the computer's hard drive.

screen: VDT.

scrolling: movement of text up and down on the screen by using the mouse or arrow keys.

shadow: accidental, partial depression or striking of a steno machine key.

total access courtroom: a courtroom that has the available equipment to allow a real-time feed to be seen on computer monitors for hearing impaired jurors.

transcript reduction: software which enables the reporter to print out four to six transcript pages into a single hardcopy.

universal dictionary: a dictionary of words created by a computer vendor.

untranslate: an outline that the computer does not have an English interpretation or equivalent.

video text integration: the reporters link to a real-time feed to a video recording.

videoconferencing: a media that allows people to meet through an interactive video link despite long physical distances of separation.

voice recognition technology: the software that allows people to talk into a microphone and have their words printed onto the screen automatically.

Westlaw: an online legal database.

How to Overcome Test Anxiety

Just the thought of taking a test is enough to make most people a little nervous. A test is an important event that can have a long-term impact on your future, so it's important to take it seriously and it's natural to feel anxious about performing well. But just because anxiety is normal, that doesn't mean that it's helpful in test taking, or that you should simply accept it as part of your life. Anxiety can have a variety of effects. These effects can be mild, like making you feel slightly nervous, or severe, like blocking your ability to focus or remember even a simple detail.

If you experience test anxiety—whether severe or mild—it's important to know how to beat it. To discover this, first you need to understand what causes test anxiety.

Causes of Test Anxiety

While we often think of anxiety as an uncontrollable emotional state, it can actually be caused by simple, practical things. One of the most common causes of test anxiety is that a person does not feel adequately prepared for their test. This feeling can be the result of many different issues such as poor study habits or lack of organization, but the most common culprit is time management. Starting to study too late, failing to organize your study time to cover all of the material, or being distracted while you study will mean that you're not well prepared for the test. This may lead to cramming the night before, which will cause you to be physically and mentally exhausted for the test. Poor time management also contributes to feelings of stress, fear, and hopelessness as you realize you are not well prepared but don't know what to do about it.

Other times, test anxiety is not related to your preparation for the test but comes from unresolved fear. This may be a past failure on a test, or poor performance on tests in general. It may come from comparing yourself to others who seem to be performing better or from the stress of living up to expectations. Anxiety may be driven by fears of the future—how failure on this test would affect your educational and career goals. These fears are often completely irrational, but they can still negatively impact your test performance.

Elements of Test Anxiety

As mentioned earlier, test anxiety is considered to be an emotional state, but it has physical and mental components as well. Sometimes you may not even realize that you are suffering from test anxiety until you notice the physical symptoms. These can include trembling hands, rapid heartbeat, sweating, nausea, and tense muscles. Extreme anxiety may lead to fainting or vomiting. Obviously, any of these symptoms can have a negative impact on testing. It is important to recognize them as soon as they begin to occur so that you can address the problem before it damages your performance.

The mental components of test anxiety include trouble focusing and inability to remember learned information. During a test, your mind is on high alert, which can help you recall information and stay focused for an extended period of time. However, anxiety interferes with your mind's natural processes, causing you to blank out, even on the questions you know well. The strain of testing during anxiety makes it difficult to stay focused, especially on a test that may take several hours. Extreme anxiety can take a huge mental toll, making it difficult not only to recall test information but even to understand the test questions or pull your thoughts together.

Effects of Test Anxiety

Test anxiety is like a disease—if left untreated, it will get progressively worse. Anxiety leads to poor performance, and this reinforces the feelings of fear and failure, which in turn lead to poor performances on subsequent tests. It can grow from a mild nervousness to a crippling condition. If allowed to progress, test anxiety can have a big impact on your schooling, and consequently on your future.

Test anxiety can spread to other parts of your life. Anxiety on tests can become anxiety in any stressful situation, and blanking on a test can turn into panicking in a job situation. But fortunately, you don't have to let anxiety rule your testing and determine your grades. There are a number of relatively simple steps you can take to move past anxiety and function normally on a test and in the rest of life.

Physical Steps for Beating Test Anxiety

While test anxiety is a serious problem, the good news is that it can be overcome. It doesn't have to control your ability to think and remember information. While it may take time, you can begin taking steps today to beat anxiety.

Just as your first hint that you may be struggling with anxiety comes from the physical symptoms, the first step to treating it is also physical. Rest is crucial for having a clear, strong mind. If you are tired, it is much easier to give in to anxiety. But if you establish good sleep habits, your body and mind will be ready to perform optimally, without the strain of exhaustion. Additionally, sleeping well helps you to retain information better, so you're more likely to recall the answers when you see the test questions.

Getting good sleep means more than going to bed on time. It's important to allow your brain time to relax. Take study breaks from time to time so it doesn't get overworked, and don't study right before bed. Take time to rest your mind before trying to rest your body, or you may find it difficult to fall asleep.

Along with sleep, other aspects of physical health are important in preparing for a test. Good nutrition is vital for good brain function. Sugary foods and drinks may give a burst of energy but this burst is followed by a crash, both physically and emotionally. Instead, fuel your body with protein and vitamin-rich foods.

Also, drink plenty of water. Dehydration can lead to headaches and exhaustion, especially if your brain is already under stress from the rigors of the test. Particularly if your test is a long one, drink water during the breaks. And if possible, take an energy-boosting snack to eat between sections.

Along with sleep and diet, a third important part of physical health is exercise. Maintaining a steady workout schedule is helpful, but even taking 5-minute study breaks to walk can help get your blood pumping faster and clear your head. Exercise also releases endorphins, which contribute to a positive feeling and can help combat test anxiety.

When you nurture your physical health, you are also contributing to your mental health. If your body is healthy, your mind is much more likely to be healthy as well. So take time to rest, nourish your body with healthy food and water, and get moving as much as possible. Taking these physical steps will make you stronger and more able to take the mental steps necessary to overcome test anxiety.

Mental Steps for Beating Test Anxiety

Working on the mental side of test anxiety can be more challenging, but as with the physical side, there are clear steps you can take to overcome it. As mentioned earlier, test anxiety often stems from lack of preparation, so the obvious solution is to prepare for the test. Effective studying may be the most important weapon you have for beating test anxiety, but you can and should employ several other mental tools to combat fear.

First, boost your confidence by reminding yourself of past success—tests or projects that you aced. If you're putting as much effort into preparing for this test as you did for those, there's no reason you should expect to fail here. Work hard to prepare; then trust your preparation.

Second, surround yourself with encouraging people. It can be helpful to find a study group, but be sure that the people you're around will encourage a positive attitude. If you spend time with others who are anxious or cynical, this will only contribute to your own anxiety. Look for others who are motivated to study hard from a desire to succeed, not from a fear of failure.

Third, reward yourself. A test is physically and mentally tiring, even without anxiety, and it can be helpful to have something to look forward to. Plan an activity following the test, regardless of the outcome, such as going to a movie or getting ice cream.

When you are taking the test, if you find yourself beginning to feel anxious, remind yourself that you know the material. Visualize successfully completing the test. Then take a few deep, relaxing breaths and return to it. Work through the questions carefully but with confidence, knowing that you are capable of succeeding.

Developing a healthy mental approach to test taking will also aid in other areas of life. Test anxiety affects more than just the actual test—it can be damaging to your mental health and even contribute to depression. It's important to beat test anxiety before it becomes a problem for more than testing.

Study Strategy

Being prepared for the test is necessary to combat anxiety, but what does being prepared look like? You may study for hours on end and still not feel prepared. What you need is a strategy for test prep. The next few pages outline our recommended steps to help you plan out and conquer the challenge of preparation.

Step 1: Scope Out the Test

Learn everything you can about the format (multiple choice, essay, etc.) and what will be on the test. Gather any study materials, course outlines, or sample exams that may be available. Not only will this help you to prepare, but knowing what to expect can help to alleviate test anxiety.

Step 2: Map Out the Material

Look through the textbook or study guide and make note of how many chapters or sections it has. Then divide these over the time you have. For example, if a book has 15 chapters and you have five days to study, you need to cover three chapters each day. Even better, if you have the time, leave an extra day at the end for overall review after you have gone through the material in depth.

If time is limited, you may need to prioritize the material. Look through it and make note of which sections you think you already have a good grasp on, and which need review. While you are studying, skim quickly through the familiar sections and take more time on the challenging parts.

Write out your plan so you don't get lost as you go. Having a written plan also helps you feel more in control of the study, so anxiety is less likely to arise from feeling overwhelmed at the amount to cover.

Step 3: Gather Your Tools

Decide what study method works best for you. Do you prefer to highlight in the book as you study and then go back over the highlighted portions? Or do you type out notes of the important information? Or is it helpful to make flashcards that you can carry with you? Assemble the pens, index cards, highlighters, post-it notes, and any other materials you may need so you won't be distracted by getting up to find things while you study.

If you're having a hard time retaining the information or organizing your notes, experiment with different methods. For example, try color-coding by subject with colored pens, highlighters, or post-it notes. If you learn better by hearing, try recording yourself reading your notes so you can listen while in the car, working out, or simply sitting at your desk. Ask a friend to quiz you from your flashcards, or try teaching someone the material to solidify it in your mind.

Step 4: Create Your Environment

It's important to avoid distractions while you study. This includes both the obvious distractions like visitors and the subtle distractions like an uncomfortable chair (or a too-comfortable couch that makes you want to fall asleep). Set up the best study environment possible: good lighting and a comfortable work area. If background music helps you focus, you may want to turn it on, but otherwise keep the room quiet. If you are using a computer to take notes, be sure you don't have any other windows open, especially applications like social media, games, or anything else that could distract you. Silence your phone and turn off notifications. Be sure to keep water close by so you stay hydrated while you study (but avoid unhealthy drinks and snacks).

Also, take into account the best time of day to study. Are you freshest first thing in the morning? Try to set aside some time then to work through the material. Is your mind clearer in the afternoon or evening? Schedule your study session then. Another method is to study at the same time of day that you will take the test, so that your brain gets used to working on the material at that time and will be ready to focus at test time.

Step 5: Study!

Once you have done all the study preparation, it's time to settle into the actual studying. Sit down, take a few moments to settle your mind so you can focus, and begin to follow your study plan. Don't give in to distractions or let yourself procrastinate. This is your time to prepare so you'll be ready to fearlessly approach the test. Make the most of the time and stay focused.

Of course, you don't want to burn out. If you study too long you may find that you're not retaining the information very well. Take regular study breaks. For example, taking five minutes out of every hour to walk briskly, breathing deeply and swinging your arms, can help your mind stay fresh.

As you get to the end of each chapter or section, it's a good idea to do a quick review. Remind yourself of what you learned and work on any difficult parts. When you feel that you've mastered the material, move on to the next part. At the end of your study session, briefly skim through your notes again.

But while review is helpful, cramming last minute is NOT. If at all possible, work ahead so that you won't need to fit all your study into the last day. Cramming overloads your brain with more information than it can process and retain, and your tired mind may struggle to recall even previously learned information when it is overwhelmed with last-minute study. Also, the urgent nature of cramming and the stress placed on your brain contribute to anxiety. You'll be more likely to go to the test feeling unprepared and having trouble thinking clearly.

So don't cram, and don't stay up late before the test, even just to review your notes at a leisurely pace. Your brain needs rest more than it needs to go over the information again. In fact, plan to finish your studies by noon or early afternoon the day before the test. Give your brain the rest of the day to relax or focus on other things, and get a good night's sleep. Then you will be fresh for the test and better able to recall what you've studied.

Step 6: Take a Practice Test

Many courses offer sample tests, either online or in the study materials. This is an excellent resource to check whether you have mastered the material, as well as to prepare for the test format and environment.

Check the test format ahead of time: the number of questions, the type (multiple choice, free response, etc.), and the time limit. Then create a plan for working through them. For example, if you have 30 minutes to take a 60-question test, your limit is 30 seconds per question. Spend less time on the questions you know well so that you can take more time on the difficult ones.

If you have time to take several practice tests, take the first one open book, with no time limit. Work through the questions at your own pace and make sure you fully understand them. Gradually work up to taking a test under test conditions: sit at a desk with all study materials put away and set a timer. Pace yourself to make sure you finish the test with time to spare and go back to check your answers if you have time.

After each test, check your answers. On the questions you missed, be sure you understand why you missed them. Did you misread the question (tests can use tricky wording)? Did you forget the information? Or was it something you hadn't learned? Go back and study any shaky areas that the practice tests reveal.

Taking these tests not only helps with your grade, but also aids in combating test anxiety. If you're already used to the test conditions, you're less likely to worry about it, and working through tests until you're scoring well gives you a confidence boost. Go through the practice tests until you feel comfortable, and then you can go into the test knowing that you're ready for it.

Test Tips

On test day, you should be confident, knowing that you've prepared well and are ready to answer the questions. But aside from preparation, there are several test day strategies you can employ to maximize your performance.

First, as stated before, get a good night's sleep the night before the test (and for several nights before that, if possible). Go into the test with a fresh, alert mind rather than staying up late to study.

Try not to change too much about your normal routine on the day of the test. It's important to eat a nutritious breakfast, but if you normally don't eat breakfast at all, consider eating just a protein bar. If you're a coffee drinker, go ahead and have your normal coffee. Just make sure you time it so that the caffeine doesn't wear off right in the middle of your test. Avoid sugary beverages, and drink enough water to stay hydrated but not so much that you need a restroom break 10 minutes into the test. If your test isn't first thing in the morning, consider going for a walk or doing a light workout before the test to get your blood flowing.

Allow yourself enough time to get ready, and leave for the test with plenty of time to spare so you won't have the anxiety of scrambling to arrive in time. Another reason to be early is to select a good seat. It's helpful to sit away from doors and windows, which can be distracting. Find a good seat, get out your supplies, and settle your mind before the test begins.

When the test begins, start by going over the instructions carefully, even if you already know what to expect. Make sure you avoid any careless mistakes by following the directions.

Then begin working through the questions, pacing yourself as you've practiced. If you're not sure on an answer, don't spend too much time on it, and don't let it shake your confidence. Either skip it and come back later, or eliminate as many wrong answers as possible and guess among the remaining ones. Don't dwell on these questions as you continue—put them out of your mind and focus on what lies ahead.

Be sure to read all of the answer choices, even if you're sure the first one is the right answer. Sometimes you'll find a better one if you keep reading. But don't second-guess yourself if you do immediately know the answer. Your gut instinct is usually right. Don't let test anxiety rob you of the information you know.

If you have time at the end of the test (and if the test format allows), go back and review your answers. Be cautious about changing any, since your first instinct tends to be correct, but make sure you didn't misread any of the questions or accidentally mark the wrong answer choice. Look over any you skipped and make an educated guess.

At the end, leave the test feeling confident. You've done your best, so don't waste time worrying about your performance or wishing you could change anything. Instead, celebrate the successful completion of this test. And finally, use this test to learn how to deal with anxiety even better next time.

Review Video: Test Anxiety
Visit mometrix.com/academy and enter code: 100340

Important Qualification

Not all anxiety is created equal. If your test anxiety is causing major issues in your life beyond the classroom or testing center, or if you are experiencing troubling physical symptoms related to your anxiety, it may be a sign of a serious physiological or psychological condition. If this sounds like your situation, we strongly encourage you to seek professional help.

Online Resources

Due to our efforts to try to keep this book to a manageable length, we've created a link that will give you access to all of your online resources:

mometrix.com/resources719/courtreporter

It's Your Moment, Let's Celebrate It!

Share your story @mometrixtestpreparation